Surprise!
YOU'RE A
LANDLORD

A Guide to
Renting Your Home
When You Didn't Expect To

Surprise!
YOU'RE A
LANDLORD

John A. Yoegel, PhD, DREI

AVON, MASSACHUSETTS

Published by Adams Business,
an imprint of Adams Media,
a division of F+W Media, Inc.
57 Littlefield Street, Avon, MA 02322. U.S.A.
www.adamsmedia.com

ISBN 10: 1-60550-637-0
ISBN 13: 978-1-60550-637-1

Printed in Canada.

J I H G F E D C B A

Library of Congress Cataloging-in-Publication Data
is available from the publisher.

This publication is designed to provide accurate and authoritative information
with regard to the subject matter covered. It is sold with the understanding that
the publisher is not engaged in rendering legal, accounting, or other professional
advice. If legal advice or other expert assistance is required, the services of a competent professional person should be sought.
　　　—From a *Declaration of Principles* jointly adopted by a Committee of the
American Bar Association and a Committee of Publishers and Associations

Many of the designations used by manufacturers and sellers to distinguish their
product are claimed as trademarks. Where those designations appear in this book
and Adams Media was aware of a trademark claim, the designations have been
printed with initial capital letters.

This book is available at quantity discounts for bulk purchases.
For information, please call 1-800-289-0963.

This book is dedicated to my wife, Marina.

*My hope is that the readers of this book will
be as grateful to her as I am for her support
of my career as an author and teacher.*

CONTENTS

Part Two. *continued*

Acknowledgments

FIRST I WOULD like to thank all my students. It is truly an unusual day in the classroom when I don't learn something from them. My continued gratitude goes to my agent, Grace Freedson, who keeps me busy enough at the computer that after five books I'm really beginning to believe I may have a career as an author. Finally I wish to thank the staff at Adams Media. Authors always know who it is that makes them look good after they've written their book.

INTRODUCTION

THIS BOOK IS written for anyone who owns a one-family house, condominium, or cooperative and wants to rent it. The material is as complete as possible to guide you, the first-time landlord, through the rental process. It is in some ways a primer on becoming a landlord. Though not its primary focus, this book may also serve as an introduction to the would-be real estate investor and property manager. If you find this material interesting and want additional information, there are a number of references at the end of this book that you might find helpful.

But for now, you have unexpectedly found that you are, or are about to become, a landlord. Landlording can be fun, exciting, challenging, and profitable. One thing it won't be is dull. The material in this book should make the experience understandable and rewarding.

Please note two things as you begin reading. First, this is a relatively short book for the subject covered. Jump around a bit if you like, but each section has important material you should be aware of if you are going to be a landlord.

Second, this is not a legal book. It is inevitable in any book about real estate that legal matters will be discussed, but the purpose of the book is not to provide legal advice. You should consult an attorney before signing any legal documents or pursuing any legal action or other activity that may result in a legal action, such as an eviction or a lawsuit. The same advice applies to accounting issues and the use of qualified accountants to advise you on the various tax and financial issues associated with owning and managing a rental property.

So now that you have gotten past the surprise of becoming a landlord, let's get started on becoming the most successful landlord you can be.

Part One

SO NOW YOU'RE A LANDLORD

CHAPTER ONE
RENTING YOUR HOUSE

YOU'VE GOT SOME decisions to make and here are a few things to consider as you make those decisions.

How Did I Get Here and What Do I Do Now?

You're faced with being a landlord because you want to sell your house* and can't. And you have to move. Or it makes economic sense to move now. Maybe you've inherited a house and it's not a good time to sell. Whatever the circumstances, you're thinking about renting your house until the market or your own situation changes enough to allow you to sell it.

Why can't you sell your house? Maybe there are a great many foreclosures in your neighborhood. Perhaps a major industry left your city and there are more houses on the market than there are buyers. It may be possible to sell your house but not at the price you want. Maybe you've tried to sell your house but the offers you're getting will not cover your outstanding mortgage balance.

If you can't sell your house, why move? Maybe you have to take that new job in another city and the kids have to start school. Perhaps you can't afford the mortgage payments anymore. Your adjustable

---

Note to the reader: Throughout this book the terms *house* and *property* are used interchangeably as is typical in the real estate business. When referring to the land portion of your property, such as when discussing lawn maintenance, the term *land* will be used. The term *house* will be used generically to mean single-family home, condominium, or cooperative.

rate mortgage adjusted beyond what you can pay, or perhaps you were downsized from your job. And if you are lucky enough to have inherited a house, you might be in an economic situation where it makes sense to wait until conditions change before you sell it.

Whatever the reason, you're faced with owning a house that you can't live in and may have difficulty selling. Renting the house and becoming a landlord, although it's something you never expected or intended to do, may just be the answer to your problem.

Pros of renting a house you're going to sell

There are always pros to renting property. Some are unique to one-family houses as rental property; some apply specifically to property that you intend to sell; and at least one is dependent on the local real estate market.

- You will receive money while the property is on the market.
- You may be able to rent the property for enough money to pay the mortgage and taxes and avoid foreclosure.
- There are tax advantages to owning rental property.
- The property will not be left vacant, a positive for security purposes.
- Risks of damage from frozen water pipes, a broken furnace, and a flooded basement will be minimized.
- Certain maintenance tasks can be built into the lease agreement.
- The tenant may turn out to be the buyer.

Cons of renting a house you're going to sell

The overall negative for some people of renting a house is the responsibility of being a landlord. But beyond that there are some negatives particularly related to property that is being rented in anticipation of selling it.

- Tenants certainly vary, but no one will take care of your house better than you will.

- Tenant abuse of the property may result in redecorating and repair expenditures before it is once again ready to market.
- Tenants are entitled to their privacy, so showing the property to prospective buyers may sometimes be difficult.
- An unhappy tenant or one who wishes to remain in the house as a tenant may speak negatively about the house to prospective buyers.
- A buyer in a hurry to move in may be reluctant to purchase your house since they will have to wait until the tenant moves out.
- Eviction proceedings may be necessary to deliver the house vacant to a buyer.

Some of these negatives will be discussed in later sections of the book.

Pros of being a landlord

The issues involved in being a landlord are similar to those of renting property, but are more personal to you.

- If you've ever thought about owning rental property as an investment, now is the time to find out if it's for you without having to buy property.
- Owning and managing rental property is a multifaceted experience from which you can learn a lot about negotiation, property values, and real estate markets.
- Tax benefits may be available to you as a landlord if you manage the property yourself.
- You have little to lose and potentially a lot to gain, especially if the mortgage on the property is a financial strain.

Cons of being a landlord

- Directly managing a rental property can be a 24/7 job.
- There is not enough headache medicine in the world if you have a bad tenant.

- Renting property is not without financial risk. Tenants can damage your property so badly as to create a net loss relative to rental income.
- You may have to pay for an attorney in the event of an eviction.

HAVE TO MOVE. WHAT TO DO?

Fred and Sally have lived in their house for five years and now want to sell their house and move to a city closer to where both their parents live. At the time they started thinking about this plan, the housing market was starting to level off but was still pretty steady. A lot has changed in the past year. They could sell if they dropped their asking price enough, but that would mean taking a loss. And they had hoped for at least a small profit to help them with a down payment on a new house.

Oddly enough, it seems that the rental market is still pretty strong in their community. Fred and Sally have spoken to their parents; both have houses with some extra room. Moving in with one of their families might allow them to save a little money. Renting their house to cover all or most of their bills may be the temporary answer to making their move and not losing their shirts.

The Professional Property Manager Option

The use of a paid property manager is discussed in detail later in this book, but following are some of the issues you need to consider in deciding whether or not to manage the property yourself:

Can the property be rented for enough to offset the cost of a property manager?

If you have later intentions of investing in real estate, know that most small residential properties do not generate enough money to pay a manager. This may be the golden opportunity to try out landlording.

Do you want to be a landlord?

Are you going to be living close enough to the property to be able to manage it yourself?

Will you be able to find a suitable property manager for what you hope will be a short-term assignment managing one property?

Judge the Market

You're faced with the decision to rent your house because the market is not "cooperating" in your efforts to sell it. You may believe that if you wait, the market will improve. Here are a few truths about real estate markets and selling a house:

One can only speak with certainty about any market—real estate, stocks, antique furniture, or baseball cards—in the past and the present, not the future.

Speculations about the future are just speculations, even if they are made by knowledgeable and experienced people.

With rare exceptions, a property does not sell in a timely fashion because it is priced too high for the current market.

While no one can predict the future, gather information about the current market and use it to make the best decision possible right now.

Renting your house while you wait to sell it may be a wise move. It may actually net you a profit. Or it can simply increase your losses. The decision to rent while you try to sell your house is based primarily on an unknown future market situation. All you can do is make the best decision based on information available now.

A Little Research and Math to Help You Make a Decision

"Real Estate Math," Chapter 19, discusses facts and figures you might want to research to help you make a decision about renting your house. There's also some simple math that will help you analyze the market. It won't show you how to predict the future, but you may be able to understand the present a little better.

You Have a Place to Live

This may seem obvious, but if you're deciding whether or not to rent your house you need to consider where you will be living in the meantime. The choices are pretty straightforward and will be determined in part by your own family situation and your economic circumstances. Here are some choices and the issues involved:

New home

Your finances are such that you have been able to purchase a new home with or without a mortgage while still owning your old house.

Renting a new home with the option to purchase

You've identified the house you'd like to buy and can persuade the owner to allow you to rent it until you sell your old house and have the money to purchase the new one.

Second or retirement home

You already own a second home or a retirement home. Perhaps it was always your intention to move to this house or your work is such that you can move to the second home temporarily. Depending on the specific circumstances, there may be tax benefits in making this kind of move.

Renting a house or apartment

Assuming that you must move to a new location and can't afford to purchase a new home until you sell the old one, renting may be the only option. Chapter 19 will help you analyze the financial issues involved in this alternative.

Moving in with family

This alternative is becoming popular and in some cases necessary where financial considerations are driving the decision to sell the house. There are a number of circumstances that may make this decision practical:

You can no longer afford your mortgage and property tax payments.

You must remain in the area due to job and/or family considerations.

You have family (or friends) who would be willing to allow you to stay with them for an undetermined period of time.

The numbers work (please see Chapter 19 for a specific analysis).

Renting Your House Furnished or Unfurnished

If you rent your house while you try to sell it or while you wait for the market to improve, you will need to decide whether to rent it furnished or unfurnished. As with most things, there are positives and negatives to either choice.

If you rent it furnished:

- Assuming you will continue to market the property while you're renting it, buyers will see your taste in decorating, not your tenant's.
- You can offer the property to relatively short-term renters who need temporary housing. This may make it easier to move them out when the time comes.
- If you are not moving to a new house or apartment, you will save on storage costs.
- If you move to temporary quarters that are furnished, you'll save on having to move your furniture twice.
- Your furniture may be damaged or stolen by the tenants.

If you rent it unfurnished:

- Your new home or apartment, whether temporary or permanent, will need to accommodate your furniture, unless you sell it or pay for storage.
- You may have to pay for moving your furniture twice.
- If you're moving in with family, you may be able to store your furniture at no cost in someone's garage or basement.
- Your tenants may have furniture that does not show the property to its best advantage.
- You will have to rent to people who have furniture and may be looking for a long-term rental.

Do I Have What It Takes to Be a Landlord?

Skills and responsibilities of managing your rental property include:

Availability

Emergencies do not occur on schedule. You must be available twenty-four hours a day, seven days a week to respond to physical emergencies such as broken furnaces and leaking water pipes.

Dealing with tenants

This will be covered in greater detail in a later section, but renting property is about finding, dealing with, and possibly removing tenants. Even if you could find the most ideal tenant in the world, you may still prefer not to deal in negotiations of any kind.

Responsibility and control

If you are going to stay awake nights worrying about what the tenants are doing to your house or worrying about the responsibility of having a tenant, then you may not be landlord material.

The ideal candidate

If, on the other hand, you like negotiating with people, are interested in learning about managing a property, can be direct without being aggressive, and can take leaky water pipes at three o'clock in the morning in stride, then you may make an excellent landlord.

Family Support

This section is included immediately after the discussion of what it takes to be a landlord because family support for this decision is important. A few things that may affect your family in making the decision to rent your house include:

Can members of the family, such as your spouse or older children, help with managing the property?

Are the temporary living arrangements—apartment, family, friends—acceptable to your family?

Will the family be supportive of the time you need to rent and manage the property?

These may not be make-or-break considerations. And if dire financial considerations are driving the rental decision, everyone may have to agree to sacrifices. But if you have a choice, it is important that the stress caused by the inability to sell your house is not compounded by a family disagreement about what to do next.

Get the Right Information

There is some basic information that you should have as you decide whether it's practical to rent your house. Determine the average rent for a house like yours, the average time a tenant expects to remain a renter, whether the property should be furnished or unfurnished, and the commissions or fees you'll incur if you use a real estate agent to rent your property.

The best sources of this kind of information are local real estate agents, professional property managers, and rental ads in local newspapers. Information may also be available on Internet websites, but accuracy and availability vary widely.

CHAPTER ONE ACTION POINTS

☐ Consider the unique pros and cons of renting out space that you want to sell.

☐ Honestly address the pros and cons of being a landlord and whether or not you have what it takes to do the job.

☐ Decide if you physically will be able to manage the property from a time and location aspect or if you should hire a professional property manager.

☐ Determine where you're going to live while you rent your house.

☐ Decide if you will rent the house furnished or unfurnished.

☐ Do the math and consider the market for sale and rental, and make sure the numbers make sense.

☐ Consider how your family feels about all this.

CHAPTER TWO

TEMPORARY DOES NOT MEAN AMATEUR:
A FEW BUSINESS TIPS

YOU'VE MADE THE decision to rent your house either while continuing to market it or while you wait for the real estate market to improve. This may be your first experience renting property and although you intend this to be a temporary situation, there's every reason for you to start thinking like an investor/property manager.

Conflicting Goals: Renting Versus Selling

A property manager attempts to maximize income from the property while increasing or at least maintaining its value. While these goals should not conflict, they may in your case. For example, a property manager expects a certain amount of wear and tear on the property. You, on the other hand, want to minimize wear and tear since it diminishes the value of the property. So it might be prudent to take a lower-than-market rent for a tenant who will take better care of the property or who will be particularly cooperative about showing the property to prospective buyers.

A property manager likes long-term tenants since there is less concern about constantly advertising and finding new tenants. In your situation, depending on when you'll be able to sell the property, you may want short-term tenants since you'll have to deliver the property vacant to the buyer.

The tenants themselves may have a goal that conflicts with yours. They want to be tenants and you want to sell the property.

13

The next chapter will discuss in detail various tenant issues and how to accommodate these potentially conflicting goals.

A BUSINESS OR NOT A BUSINESS—THAT IS THE QUESTION
Once there were two couples, Jim and Pat and Rich and Sandy. Both couples decided to rent their houses until the market improved enough for them to sell. Rich and Sandy contacted an attorney and their accountant. They found a standard lease form and reviewed it with their attorney. They wrote up a business plan including a projected budget. Jim and Pat did none of these things.

Later both couples sold their houses. Rich and Sandy's sale went smoothly, their tenant moved out on time, and they had all the necessary records to give to their accountant for tax purposes. Jim and Pat's tenant refused to move because there was no termination clause in the lease. They had to reduce their selling price because the tenant parked his boat on the lawn. Nothing in the lease prevented this. At tax time they had to scramble to figure out what their rental income and expenses had been.

You need to decide whether you want to be Rich and Sandy or Jim and Pat.

Business Not Friends—Friendly Not Personal

We all want to be liked. But your goals as a landlord are to find good tenants, manage the property well, protect the value of the property, and ultimately, to sell the property.

Being liked by your tenants is far down on your list of priorities. Your tenants will respect you if you are honest and fair, deliver what you promise, and are very clear about your expectations of your tenants.

The best way to achieve this is to think of yourself as a property manager working for the owner of the property. As you negotiate the lease, respond to a complaint, or have to enforce some provision in the lease, think of how a property manager would do the job. The manager would remain businesslike and would avoid allowing personal feelings to affect his or her behavior. This may be easier said than done, since this is your home.

Do not get personally involved with your tenant. You must use your judgment of course, but that cup of coffee you have every month when you collect the rent may be interpreted differently by your tenants than by you. When they need a little more time to pay the rent or want to have their daughter's wedding in your backyard, they will why wonder their nice landlord said no. And they will be angry about it. Not because you did anything wrong but because they had different expectations of you.

Be courteous, respectful, friendly, and consistent in your dealings with your tenants from the first interview to the time they move out. Every decision you make and every action you take should be consistent with the dual goals of renting the property for maximum short-term advantage and in the long term, selling the property at the highest possible price.

Favors: Once Extended Hard to Take Back

There are some things that happen when renting one-family houses that can lead to difficulty. Houses generally attract families as tenants. There is nothing wrong with families as such, and as you'll see later, they enjoy the protection of fair housing laws. The issue is that the combination of a family and a one-family house can lead to favors, or worse, presumptions.

Say, for example, you have a house on a relatively large piece of property; the tenant asks if they can have their annual family reunion in the backyard and you say yes. After the fact, you find out that they have family coming from thirty states and four countries; that they will be setting up several tents and outdoor toilets; and that it will take a season for your lawn to recover from everyone parking on it. And worse, six months later, they don't even ask when they decide to have their daughter's wedding in the backyard, because, after all, you already gave them permission to have outdoor parties on the property.

Or you have a covered inground swimming pool that you do not wish to use or maintain while the property is being rented. This has been made clear in the lease. But you give in to the tenant's request to use the pool after receiving assurances that they will maintain, clean, and cover it at the end of the season; of course, they don't.

The list of what-ifs is almost endless: large parties, furniture storage, use of parts of the house or property not in the lease, extra tenants not in the lease, boat and recreational vehicle storage, and so on. Any and all of these things can be dealt with either in the lease or as a business arrangement. For example, you could ask the tenant who wants to use the swimming pool to pay a surcharge on the rent for pool maintenance, or ask the reunion family to post some type of security to repair any damage to the property. It is important that these requests be handled as business issues and not favors. "Just this once" has a way of becoming more than once.

Written Communication

Written communication is a two-edged sword. It equally provides a record of what you want recorded and what you may not want recorded. Written communication is generally viewed as formal, official, and businesslike. In property management situations, it can be used to convey legal documents such as a copy of the lease. It can help convey the seriousness of trying to obtain a desired effect, such as a letter advising the tenant of a noise complaint by the neighbors. Sometimes written communications are used to provide a record of a conversation in the event of future legal action.

However, avoid putting a threat in writing without the advice of an attorney. Perhaps you've verbally asked your tenant to stop doing something that is a violation of the lease and you've made a note of that conversation in your file. You've written to them after they did it again. After the third time you're ready to evict them. Now is the time to call your attorney even if you're not actually ready to begin eviction proceedings, but simply want to threaten them with such an action.

You may want to consult an attorney before asking the tenant to do or not do something that was not previously covered in the lease.

Attorneys

Renting a property is a contractual transaction, even if there is no written lease. Legally, you are free to represent yourself in any transaction. However, it is always advisable to consult with an attorney before signing any legal document like a lease. An alternative is to use a lease form that has been approved by an attorney or the local bar association. In that case all you would be doing is filling out factual information like name and amount of rent.

Most states require that a valid real estate transaction be in writing. Rules vary by state, and in some cases an exception is made for leases shorter than a certain term such as one year. An attorney can be invaluable in advising you of what to sign and when.

Consult an attorney if eviction proceedings become necessary to remove a tenant. Any communications, especially those in writing, involving threats of eviction or other legal action should either be prepared by an attorney or at least reviewed by an attorney if you choose to prepare them yourself.

Finally, if there is any doubt in your mind about taking some action or signing something involving the leasing of your property, it is prudent to first consult with a real estate attorney.

Accountants

As you make the decision to rent your house, consult an accountant familiar with real estate matters. Unlike an owner-occupied home, a rental property is a business. As a business, it is subject to income taxes and you may benefit from certain deductions. The tax regulations governing rental property can be complicated and you don't want to break the law or miss out on any deductions or tax benefits for which you may be eligible.

It is important to consult with an accountant as you begin the process of renting your house. Ask the accountant to specify the records you should keep, to explain the income tax implications of renting your property, and to advise you on all eligible deductions or credits.

The accountant will most likely advise you to set up a separate account to collect the rent and pay property bills, and to maintain some type of record book regarding expenditures. Because certain deductions may be available to you for managing the property yourself, you may also wish to keep a diary or calendar of your activities related to managing the property.

Tax policy regarding rental property will be discussed later, but be aware that federal tax policy and interpretations of the law change from time to time. And it would be impossible to provide information on individual state tax laws in the space of this book. Therefore, an accountant well versed in real estate matters is invaluable in providing current local and federal tax information as it affects the rental of your property.

Write a Business Plan

This may seem either foolish or a waste of time, but it will help you to think of this situation in business terms. You can research the Internet, the library, and bookstores about preparing business plans. Your plan need not be elaborate or complicated, but at a minimum the basic elements of the plan should include:

1. A simple, one-sentence statement of your goal in renting the property
2. A step-by-step implementation plan of how you will rent the property (This book will be very helpful in preparing this action plan.)
3. An operating budget
4. A capital budget if major repairs are necessary or are anticipated
5. A disposal plan of when and how you will market the house

A business plan will help you to keep on track toward your ultimate goal of selling your house, and will also help you to think like a landlord.

Consistency and Use of Forms

For your own sense of organization, ease of management, and avoidance of any fair housing complaints, it is a good idea to create or obtain standard forms for things like tenant applications, credit checks, leases, and rent collection.

You hope that your first tenant applicant has great credit and ready cash for the deposit. You also hope that the tenant stays until you sell the house and then readily moves out.

If, however, you have to screen multiple tenant applicants and/or you must re-rent the property several times before you sell it, standard forms are essential to maintain consistency, to ensure that everything is covered, and to avoid unnecessary duplication of effort.

Remember that an attorney should at least review all legal forms before you sign them.

CHAPTER TWO ACTION POINTS

☐ Write a short business plan.

☐ Find a knowledgeable real estate attorney.

☐ Find an accountant knowledgeable about real estate matters and meet to discuss the records and accounts you'll need to set up.

☐ Gather the forms you're going to use in renting your property and review them with your attorney and accountant as needed.

☐ Remind yourself that you are undertaking a business project and need to think like a landlord and property manager not a homeowner.

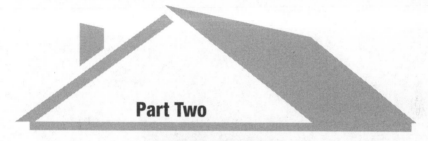

Part Two

TENANTS

AND EVERYTHING THAT COMES WITH THEM

CHAPTER THREE
THE PERFECT TENANTS: FIND THEM; KEEP THEM

YOU'VE NOW MADE the decision to rent the house while you wait to sell it. You've also decided to manage it yourself. You've lined up an attorney and an accountant; you've created a business plan including a budget. Now you're ready to find the one key element that will make you a landlord: a tenant.

Who Is the Perfect Tenant?

The perfect tenant pays her rent on time and lives somewhere else. Although that is obviously a facetious statement, it contains two elements of importance in selecting a tenant: (1) the tenant should be able to pay the rent, in full, on time, and without exception; (2) the tenant should create minimal wear and tear on the property and be a good neighbor.

Assessing financial responsibility is relatively easy. Remember, however, that you are assessing a tenant's current ability to pay. You cannot predict the possibility of that tenant losing his job or having an expensive health crisis.

The second part is perhaps the largest unpredictable risk associated with renting a house. You can minimize the risks of this situation by setting parameters for the type of tenant you want and don't want. A later chapter will discuss the legal limitations you may face in tenant selection due to fair housing laws, but within those laws you can attempt to pick the best tenant possible to rent your house.

Set Your Tenant Selection Parameters

It's possible to make some very broad generalizations about the parameters you want to consider in selecting a tenant. These generalities are not meant to stereotype or denigrate any particular group or characteristic. This is about wear and tear on the property and nothing else. And remember that there are exceptions to every situation. Please refer to Chapter 6 on fair housing laws to determine if you can make a tenant selection based on certain characteristics and if you can advertise along these lines.

In general, here are some things you may want to avoid in selecting a tenant.

Pets

Animals can be hard on a property. Do not let your own prejudices about pets affect your judgment. Animals, unless they are extremely well maintained by their owners, generally have an odor. Animals may defecate and urinate indoors and on furniture. Some animals shed. Fish tanks can break and, if not kept clean, can smell. All of these can affect carpeting, wooden floors, furniture, and drapes. The odor and dirt may belong to the tenant, but it's your house you're trying to sell.

Students

If you live in a college town, you may consider renting your house to students. Because students may rent semester by semester, you would not need to worry about a long-term lease while you're selling the property. However, can you remember your room at home when you went to school? Do you remember your dorm room? Maybe you rented a house or an apartment with some other students when you went to college. Do you remember how it looked most of the time? You probably don't remember how it smelled, because you got used to it. What makes you think that these students will treat your property any better than you or your friends did? And did I forget to mention the loud parties? Enough said.

Smoking

More and more people find the smell of cigarette, cigar, and pipe smoke to be offensive. Unfortunately, the smell of smoke eventually will permeate rugs, furniture, drapes, and perhaps even walls. Smell is an important trigger in forming positive or negative reactions. This fact gives rise to the old advice about having an apple pie baking in the oven when showing a house for sale because of the pleasant aroma.

Large families

This issue is difficult because there may be fair housing issues in play here. The point is that the greater the number of people in the house, the more wear and tear. In general, one can limit a rental to two people per bedroom. This means that you could deny renting your three-bedroom house to a family of more than six persons. Please note carefully that this rule is governed by local laws and should be checked and verified with local authorities as discussed in Chapter 7.

Home occupations

If a person is self-employed as a writer and will be using one of the bedrooms as a home office, it is unlikely that there will be any additional wear and tear on the house. On the other hand, you may want to avoid the tenant who is a car mechanic and intends to set up a side business in your garage. Local ordinances, discussed in Chapter 7, may regulate home occupations.

Hobbies

This may seem to be a stretch but in selecting a tenant inquire about hobbies. Someone who sculpts metal with an arc welding machine may pose risks for the property that an avid knitter would not.

Beyond this, as long as you stay within the law, do your best to assess the impact a particular tenant may have on your property. If you intend to market the property while it is being rented, you want a tenant who is neat and clean. If you're going to wait a while to market the property, you want a tenant who will not damage your property.

Getting the Word Out

You will have a much better chance of finding the right tenant if you can select from several applicants. And that means getting the word out. Following are ways to advertise your rental property and generate applications.

Print advertising

A good place to start advertising your rental is in the local newspaper and those of adjacent communities. For example, if you live in a suburb where many people commute into adjacent areas, an ad in those papers may attract people who want to move to your area. If you are renting a very high-priced house, you might even consider a feature ad with a photo in the magazine section of the paper if the cost is warranted.

Newspaper ads can be expensive. A cheaper alternative are the so-called shoppers' papers and magazines. They are sometimes delivered to every household by mail or can be picked up free at the supermarket. Some town weekly papers are also freely available. Advertising rates in these alternative papers are often lower than in the prime newspaper serving the town or region.

Next time you're at the local diner or supermarket, take a look to see if there are any publications specifically devoted to rentals. We're all familiar with the small free magazines that advertise homes for sale. Some of these include houses for rent and others are devoted solely to rental property. Advertising in these publications is often available only to real estate professionals, but it may be worth a call to find out if they'll take your ad.

Don't forget your company newsletter, the church bulletin, or your club newsletter, if any of these permits this type of advertising.

What should the ad say?

There are entire books written about real estate advertising. And of course every house and neighborhood is unique, so it would be difficult in a book like this to write a generic ad. After "house for rent," here are a few things to consider in writing an advertisement to rent your house:

- Note the uniquely appealing features of the house, but remember these people are renters not buyers. Space is more important than a great view or formal gardens.
- Be honest but appealing. I'm not sure anyone really knows the definition of a gourmet kitchen, but if yours is thirty years old and measures six by eight feet, it's probably not a gourmet kitchen.
- Read some other ads of houses for sale or rent and try to get an idea of what people are looking for in your neighborhood. If local ads emphasize an easy commute to a neighboring city, include that in your ad. If the ads talk about master bedroom suites and your house has one, put that in the ad.
- Mention the things you don't want. Including "no pets" or "no smoking" in your ad will allow people to eliminate themselves and save you time. Watch out for fair housing laws before you go too far in writing what or who you don't want. Generally mentioning prohibited behavior is preferable to personalizing the behavior. "No drinking" is better than "No drinkers" to avoid the possibility of misinterpretation based on stereotypes.
- In writing an ad, note that "will cooperate" means you're willing to work with a real estate broker and pay a fee if necessary. Note the broker may work on behalf of a tenant or may represent you. Who pays the fee may be subject to negotiation. "Principles only" means just the opposite. You don't want to deal with brokers; only with prospective tenants directly.

Word of mouth

Tell everyone you know that you're looking for a tenant to rent your house. Have some fact sheets printed and give them to anyone who might be interested or who knows someone who might be interested. Post a fact sheet on your company bulletin board, church or temple bulletin board, the supermarket, and anywhere else in town that has a public place to advertise things like your house for rent. Tell everyone at your club, the PTA, the choir, and any other organization you belong to.

Do not include the address of the property or your name in your print ads and flyers, especially if the house is vacant. You can put down the general neighborhood if it has a name or a geographical direction that's meaningful, such as "the west side of town" or "in the Pine Hills subdivision."

In using word of mouth, be careful to maintain your negotiating position by not revealing too much information about your reasons for renting the property. Say something like "We thought we'd rent it for a while until the market gets a little stronger." This is better than "The bank is going to foreclose and we're getting desperate."

Internet

Internet resources and sites come and go. A few that seem to have staying power are referenced in the appendix. Do a general search for sites that allow you to post properties for rent either for free or for a small fee. One obvious way is to search houses for rent as if you were a prospective tenant. If you do use Internet advertising, be sure to remove the ad after you've rented the property. Unlike newspapers, the ad may continue on the site indefinitely unless you remove it.

Relatives and friends

This group is separate because some of us like to be cautious when having business dealings with friends or family. Imagine renting your house to your sister-in-law's sister and then having to evict her or raise the rent. Proceed cautiously when sharing information with family and close friends and even more cautiously if you're thinking of renting your house to one.

> **tip**
>
> ### THE FAMILY TENANT: A CAUTIONARY TALE
>
> "I heard you're going to rent your house for a while until the market improves," says your wife's brother, Mike. "Did you know that cousin Frank is looking for a temporary place to rent?"
>
> If Frank and his family turn out to be the perfect tenants, you have lucked out and will be forever grateful to Mike.
>
> But what happens if Frank loses his job and can't pay the rent? You'll do what you would do to any tenant, ask them to leave, and evict them if necessary, right?
>
> Check the guest list for any future family functions unless you don't mind being in the same room with someone who is angry with you, including Frank and his family, his parents, brothers and sisters, and your brother-in-law who started it all.
>
> The moral of this story: Only rent to family or a friend you won't mind losing as family or a friend.

Rental agencies

Rental agencies are not real estate brokers who may specialize in rental properties, but companies that maintain lists of properties for rent. An owner can register property with the company free or for a small fee. Prospective tenants pay a fee to the company and are allowed to look at their lists for a prescribed period of time, say three months. The company provides no services as a real estate agent to either landlord or tenant.

This type of service has suffered from the reputation of those companies that do not track and delete listings that have been rented. Landlords have no motivation to call the company and take their listing off except to avoid being bothered by a call now and then from a prospective tenant. Prospective tenants therefore complain that they are often paying to look at listings that are no longer available. If there is no charge for listing the property, however, you have nothing to lose by placing it with the company.

Neighbors

Your neighbors have a vested interest in seeing your house occupied and maintained. This is especially true in a neighborhood where there have been many foreclosures or people moving without being able to sell. The neighbors also have an interest in who moves into the house. Let your neighbors know that you intend to rent the house; suggest that if they know anyone who might be interested to have them contact you.

Sign on the property

The success of a For Rent sign on the property will vary. In an area where there are few apartments and people who wish to rent a dwelling tend to rent houses, a sign will have good impact. People will drive through neighborhoods they are interested in and note houses that are being offered for rental. In an area where the typical renter rents an apartment rather than a house, a For Rent sign may be a waste of time since people driving through your neighborhood will be looking for a house to buy.

Also you need to consider whether or not you are going to continue to market the property while you are trying to rent it. You might put up a sign that says For Sale or Rent until it is rented, then switch to one that just says For Sale.

This is an area where it's important to make a distinction between a house, a condominium, and a co-op. Most associations have rules that will prevent you from putting up a sign outside your co-op or condominium. In a high-rise building, a sign would be impractical. In a low-rise garden-apartment type of building, it may be possible to place a small sign in the ground just outside the door of the unit. In any case you'll need to check the rules of the association and may need to obtain permission. Placing a For Rent sign inside a window visible from the outside may be an alternative. It is less likely to be a problem for the association but you still should check the rules.

The For Rent sign should give your phone number and nothing else.

Large companies in the area

If possible, place your rental information with the human resources or relocation departments of large companies in your area. If they agree to consider your property, send the fact sheet immediately by e-mail or fax. Employees are often transferred and may be in need of temporary housing. In some cases, particularly in corporations with international branches, temporary can mean a year or more.

Relocation companies

There are companies that specialize in providing relocation services for corporate employees. These companies often find temporary housing for transferred employees. Do an Internet search for corporate relocation companies and relocation services in your area. You can also try real estate companies that specialize in relocations. You might contact the human resources departments of larger corporations in the area and ask for the names of the relocation companies they use.

Contact the relocation company and ask if they will add your house as a possible temporary rental for one of their clients. Be prepared to indicate the length of time you'd be willing to rent your house.

Real estate brokers

Contact one or more real estate brokers and give them the rental listing for the property. In the case of rentals it is important to find out who will pay the fee and under what circumstances. In many areas the tenant and not the landlord pays rental fees, or it can be negotiated.

Most brokers will want you to sign an Exclusive Right to Lease listing agreement. This means that they will collect a fee regardless of who secures the tenant. You can also create a type of Open Listing by sending out flyers to several real estate brokers and indicating your willingness to cooperate with them and pay a fee if they find a tenant.

If you have been using a real estate broker to sell your house, speak to him first if you're going to use a broker to locate a tenant. If it is customary in your area for the landlord to pay the fee for finding a tenant, your broker may be willing to waive the fee in return for an extension of the sales listing agreement or even some assurance that when you put the house back on the market you will use him. Don't be afraid to ask for this type of courtesy arrangement if you want your real estate agent's help in finding a tenant.

Remember, that in most cases a broker makes no money unless the property gets sold. Without impugning the honesty of any particular real estate broker, you need to keep that in mind whenever you evaluate any advice your broker gives you.

Short-Term Versus Long-Term Tenants

When you select a tenant, you'll need to decide how long you expect to rent your house. There is no one right answer for every situation. Much of the decision will involve the reasons you're renting the property and your expectations of what will happen next.

Assume that you've decided to rent your house; you've rented a place to live in the town you're moving to, and plan on selling your house as soon as you can get your price. The best you can do is to make an informed guess about the market in your area. Is it stagnant or in decline? Does it appear to have bottomed out and is in a turnaround situation? Since we're speaking of dollars and cents here, you may want to check out the real estate math in Chapter 19 for a few scenarios. If you think it's likely that you're going to have to wait at least a year to sell your house, then you can safely look for a tenant who'll need a place to live for about that period of time. On the other hand if you are very motivated to sell and may be willing to drop your price a little, and the market has not been too severely affected, you may want to rent for three to six months.

You're dealing with the future, which by definition is unpredictable. If it takes you longer to sell the house than you anticipated, then you may have to rent to a series of short-term tenants, with the accompanying search and selection of a tenant repeated several times. If the house sells in less time than anticipated, you may have to evict the longer-term tenant.

Qualify Tenants—Can They Pay?

Qualify the tenant by determining if they can and will pay their monthly rent. Their ability to pay should be determined by the amount of income they receive and the source of that income. Using information on the application form, verify salary and place and length of employment. Because of increasing rules about privacy, this will most likely have to be done in writing using a permission form signed by the applicant. You can also ask for a copy of their most recent paycheck statement though that does not guarantee that they are still employed. If their income is from another source—a pension, for example—you can ask for verification by means of copies of their records and a phone call, e-mail, or letter to the source of their pension.

The rule of thumb historically used to determine how much one should pay for rent was 25 percent of gross family income. That has increased to 30 percent of gross family income for federally subsidized housing. This is a somewhat arbitrary percentage based on an estimation of what's needed for other family expenses. It's reasonable to expect that an older couple without children or with grown children could spend 35 percent of their income on rent. On the other hand, the couple with three children should probably not exceed that 25 percent number for their rent payments. Remember, too, that the renter of your house will probably pay for heat, which many apartment renters do not. If your house is large, their utility bills will be higher than for an apartment renter. So be cautious about choosing a tenant for whom the rent appears to be burdensome. You're the one who will lose rent money tenants can't pay, and it is you who will have to hire an attorney to evict them.

You can also use the typical mortgage qualifying ratio as a guideline. A bank will often allow a borrower to pay up to 28 percent of their gross income for mortgage payment, taxes, and insurance and up to 36 percent of their gross income for total long-term debt payments. It can get a little complicated applying this to a rental situation since taxes and mortgage interest are deductible for homeowners. It still is a good guideline in terms of what someone can actually pay on a month-by-month basis. If it appears that the rent will be more than 30 percent of your prospective tenants' gross income, be cautious about their ability to pay.

Qualify Tenants—Will They Pay?

You also want some assurance that the tenants will pay the rent. High income is no guarantee that tenants will pay the rent regularly and on time.

You can get the assurance you need by obtaining the tenant's credit report. This will assess their debt situation and history of payments as well as any major financial issues such as a bankruptcy. Using their application and signed consent, you will ask a credit-checking service to find their credit history. Review the credit history for any significant financial issues like a recent bankruptcy, and take note of their pattern of payment of debts. They should not be consistently late in their credit card payments, utility bills, or other regular obligations.

Finally, and this relates to the ability to pay as noted in the previous section, take a look at other debt payments the applicant has to make each month. The rent may be only 25 or 30 percent of their gross income, but if they're already paying out 40 or 50 percent in car loans or leases, credit card debts, and student loans, you may want to think carefully about renting to them.

Identity Issues

Identity theft is becoming more common and you want to make sure that your prospective tenants are who they say they are. Short of fingerprints and DNA testing, a clever criminal can probably pull off a successful identity theft in a rental situation. It's advisable to check as much information as you can about the individual. Here are a few things you can do:

- Meet the tenant in person.
- Verify that the current address provided is correct.
- Obtain a copy of the individual's driver's license or other government-issued photo ID and match up the face to the photo.
- Question any inconsistencies with respect to previous addresses or employment that appear between the application and the credit report.
- Check references in person showing the reference a copy of the photo ID.

Criminal Background

While you are checking the identity of the applicant, visit your local police department and ask if they will do a criminal background check on the applicant for you. Most likely they will not, but they may be able to refer you to a service that can perform this criminal check. If the local police can't refer you, a phone book or Internet search should locate a service that performs criminal background checks. You will have to pay a fee and the data available may not be up-to-date. If you decide to do this, you may want to limit this type of search to your final rental candidate. On the other hand, if you have verified that your prospective tenant has been continuously employed by the same employer for thirty years, has lived at the same address for all that time, and has a first-class credit history, you may want to save the cost of a criminal background check. Depending on the cost of the background check and the verifiable quality of the tenant, you'll need to decide whether to check this particular aspect of the rental applicant.

Sex Offender List

There is nothing to say that you cannot or should not rent your house to a registered sex offender. Unless your state has included these people in a protected class category, which will be discussed later, it's your choice. The responsibility for notification of neighbors that typically accompanies this status is usually the offender's. All states maintain lists of registered sex offenders, which are generally accessible on the Internet or through the local police department. If this is an issue for you, you'll need to check the applicant's name at their current and/or previous address. Remember, if they're coming from somewhere else, particularly another state, they are probably not yet registered in your state's database. Check your state and local laws to avoid violating any civil rights that may have been granted to sex offenders with respect to their privacy or other discrimination issues.

Select the Tenant

To complete the work of this chapter, you'll need to review all the information you've gathered and select your new tenant. If you are fortunate, you will have several qualified applicants to choose from. If not, you may have only one semi-qualified candidate. While you may feel the pressure of your particular financial situation, keep in mind that the best way to ensure smooth tenant relations is to make a careful selection of the tenant in the first place. Also remember that your ultimate goal is to sell your house and pay the mortgage and taxes or perhaps make a little money while you find a buyer. A tenant who destroys the property or who will not pay the rent for six months and then has to be evicted is worse than no tenant at all. At some point you'll have to take a chance and pick a tenant, but don't be rushed into a decision that you may come to regret.

CHAPTER THREE ACTION POINTS

☐ If you have a broker, talk to her about renting the property.

☐ List all the ways that you can advertise the property; review the list and decide what makes the most sense to do.

☐ Advertise the property for rent in accordance with the list you've created.

☐ Determine ahead of time how to obtain credit reports, and criminal and sex offender checks so you'll be ready to go as soon as you get a qualified applicant.

☐ Select one or two likely tenant prospects.

☐ Verify each applicant's identity and income; review credit history and criminal background (if necessary).

☐ Select the tenant.

CHAPTER FOUR
LEASES

THIS CHAPTER WILL discuss the major items in a lease and should get you thinking about the decisions you'll have to make concerning the various terms and conditions under which you're going to rent your house. You will most likely use a standard lease available in your area or one prepared by your attorney. It will include a number of so-called boilerplate clauses. These terms and conditions will constitute the agreement between you and your tenant. As with any contract, the lease is just a piece of paper and only forms the basis for legal action if either party fails to perform the promises that they have made to each other.

Remember that a standard lease form is designed simply to be filled out by the landlord and signed by both parties. If you make any changes to the standard form or wish to write your own lease, it is advisable to consult an attorney.

Term
The term of the lease is the length of time the lease is in effect. The term might read "For one year commencing on January 1, 20XX, and ending on December 31, 20XX." The term is important in any rental situation and it is especially important in your situation. In general, the term obligates the tenant and the landlord to keep the promises they make for the length of time stated. Following is a typical example of the effect of the lease term.

Let's say you have a lease with a tenant for one year. Assuming that the tenant meets all her obligations of rent payment and so on, you, the landlord, must let her remain in the property until the end of the lease. The tenant is obligated to stay in the house until the end of the lease or at least to pay the rent until the end of the lease if she chooses to leave.

Suppose you and the tenant sign a one-year lease and three months into the lease you sell the property. You cannot force the tenant to move. And unless you've sold the property to an investor, it's unlikely that a prospective buyer will close on a property with a tenant in it since the new buyer will then have to undertake removing the tenant.

On the other hand, if it takes you more than a year to sell the property and the tenant wants to move after six months, you can force her to pay out the remaining balance of the lease. As a practical matter, this is not as easy as it sounds since it may involve taking her to court and is even more difficult and expensive if she's moved to another state.

Depending on how well you think you can predict the future, you could offer the tenant a shorter-term lease, say six months. The downside to this is that you may only get a tenant who wants a six-month lease and will move out at the end of the term. If you haven't sold the property yet, you'll have to go through the entire rental process again.

This may seem a bit overwhelming, but keep in mind that this has nothing to do with good or bad tenants. Remember, selling the house is your ultimate goal. The issue of a tenant's timing and plans and the unknown date your house will sell are part of the cost of doing business in this particular case.

There are two possible alternatives to the fixed-term problem. First, you may offer the house on a month-to-month basis. This means that either party—tenant or landlord—can terminate the lease on one month's notice without further obligation. Consult an attorney for specific wording on this since there are a few variations of how this can be done. Be aware that an astute tenant will try and protect himself from a landlord using the thirty-day notice provision to simply raise the rent.

The other and perhaps preferable alternative, if agreed to by the tenant, is called a "termination on sale" clause. This means that upon sale of the property, the lease ends and the tenant has a specified number of days to vacate the house. This will serve your purposes as a landlord who is trying to sell a property and needs to turn it over vacant to a buyer. It may not serve the interests of the tenant. While the termination-on-sale clause may be your best bet, it's important to understand the other issues connected to the lease term.

When the lease term is over and a new lease is not signed, the lease becomes what is typically called a "tenancy at will," which is effectively a month-to-month tenancy. This tenancy can usually be terminated by either party upon proper notice, and is sometimes governed by state law. It is a good idea to include this provision in the lease in a specific clause after the lease term. The clause should indicate that at the end of the lease term, the tenancy will become a month-to-month tenancy under the same terms as the lease and can be terminated upon thirty days' (or other time frame) notice by either party.

Finally, when you give the lease to the new tenant, you may want to formally tell her that she should consult an attorney before she signs it. This advice will often be part of a standardized lease and should be included on any lease either you or your attorney prepares. You should, however, make a point of explaining the lease term to the tenant if you use the termination-on-sale clause or the month-to-month option. If the option you select is not acceptable to the tenant, the time to find that out is at the beginning of the landlord/tenant relationship, and not when you send the notice to vacate.

Rent

Rent is often stated in terms of the total amount due for the term of the lease but with a stipulation that it can be paid periodically. If you have a one-year lease with rent at $1,000 per month, the lease would specify that the rental amount is $12,000 due in equal monthly payments of $1,000 each month. This helps clarify that the tenant is signing an obligation to pay a total of $12,000 and not simply $1,000 per month. This format is not absolutely necessary and the rent can simply be stated on a monthly basis with the lease-term clause specifying the tenant's obligation to pay the rent for the whole term of the lease.

Utility Expenses

Based on your research outlined in Chapter 8, you will need to include other monthly financial obligations of your tenant. In most single-family house rental situations, the tenant will be responsible for expenses that are not normally included in an apartment rental. For example, in an apartment rental the landlord might normally pay for heat and water but not electricity or gas. In a house rental, the tenant will usually pay all those costs.

As a practical matter, you, as landlord, will have no control over how the tenants will use the heat (or air conditioning). They should be rewarded for their efforts at conserving heat and should have to pay if they use fuel irresponsibly. Escalating fuel costs are also an issue that can most easily be taken care of by moving the obligation on to the tenant. If the house has metered water, this cost also could be borne by the tenant.

You and the tenant will have to make appropriate contact with the various companies to transfer utility payments.

Maintenance Expenses as Part of the Rent

Maintenance expenses are negotiable as are all other costs. However, they do require a little thought before you automatically try to get the tenant to pay for them.

Maintenance matters can be divided into three categories: preventive, corrective, and routine maintenance. Preventive maintenance might include the annual furnace cleaning or water softener maintenance. It's likely that as the resident homeowner, you paid someone to do this for you. It's best to continue to assume both the financial and administrative (you get to arrange it) responsibility for this. You want the house to remain in good shape since you're going to sell it.

Corrective maintenance might include a broken furnace or a leaky toilet. In general, landlords pay for those repairs that are due to normal wear and tear and try to get the tenants to pay for repairs due to misuse or negligence. This should be spelled out in the lease.

In addition to preventive and corrective maintenance, there is what is usually called routine maintenance—such as grounds and swimming pool maintenance and snow removal. If you live in an area that has real winters, snow removal will be an issue. Snow removal from a driveway and walkways on the property is for the tenants' convenience and safety and they should pay for it, make the appropriate arrangements to get it done, or do it themselves. Most communities with sidewalks do have requirements that public sidewalks be cleared of snow by a certain time or so many hours after a snowfall has stopped. If the house were vacant, you'd have to pay for that. A stipulation that the tenant is responsible for snow removal in accordance with local regulations should be put into the lease. If the tenant wants to pay to have this done, negotiate the fee, and hire a service.

If tenants wish to use the swimming pool, they should pay for the cost of routine maintenance and not do it themselves. You want the pool clean and carefully maintained when prospective buyers come to the house.

Unless the property is quite diminutive and the landscaping minimal, it's best to build into the rent the cost of professional landscaping / lawn maintenance service. Curb appeal in selling a house is very important. People have different standards of what is acceptable maintenance. Your tenant may think cutting the grass once a month and ignoring the flower beds is acceptable maintenance. It's not if you're trying to sell the house. So hire a professional and leave it out of the hands of the tenant.

Maintenance Responsibilities

Your lease should contain appropriate provisions for all maintenance responsibilities for the property. There are no specific rules for who does what or who pays for it. Once you're into actual negotiations with the tenant, you may have to adjust your original thinking about maintenance responsibilities depending on what the tenant is able to do or pay for.

Be sure you've accounted for as many anticipated expenses as possible in your budget calculations and in the lease. Do not assume that longer-term expenses need not be covered. If you're renting your house in the Northeast in April, for example, don't ignore snow removal responsibilities because you're sure the house will be sold before the first snow. Plan for as many contingencies as you can and hope they don't come to pass. Think about who will be responsible for the following:

- Lawn and landscaping care
  - ☐ Lawn mowing
  - ☐ Flower bed care
  - ☐ Trimming bushes
  - ☐ Raking leaves
- Snow removal
  - ☐ Cleaning sidewalks of snow and ice
  - ☐ Clearing snow from the driveway
  - ☐ Clearing pathways and steps
- Minor repairs
  - ☐ Leaking faucets
  - ☐ Running toilets
  - ☐ Clogged drains and toilets
- Major repairs
  - ☐ Furnace or water heater
  - ☐ Air-conditioning equipment
  - ☐ Appliances
  - ☐ Structural repairs such as leaking roof

(continued)

- Tenant-caused repairs
  - ❏ Stopped-up toilet
  - ❏ Broken window
  - ❏ Certain types of appliance damage
  - ❏ Chipped or damaged countertops, bathroom or kitchen fixtures
- Wear-and-tear repairs
  - ❏ Damage to appliances
  - ❏ Damage to furniture in a furnished house
  - ❏ Broken or cracked sidewalks and driveways
- Preventive maintenance items
  - ❏ Furnace cleaning
  - ❏ Painting
- Routine maintenance
  - ❏ Changing air-conditioning / furnace filters
  - ❏ Draining water heater
  - ❏ Changing outside bulbs
  - ❏ Cleaning gutters

These examples are only illustrative and may or may not apply to your property.

It's critical that anything you want the tenant to pay for or do is in the lease. If it's not in the lease, you and your tenants will assume that it's your responsibility.

Responsibility for Equipment

As you are considering maintenance issues, think about who will be responsible for landlord-owned equipment used by the tenant.

Maintenance equipment is the first thing that comes to mind. If you permit the tenant to assume the responsibility for mowing the lawn and you leave your lawnmower for her use, who is responsible for the repairs to the mower if it breaks? An argument over a $100 repair bill can sour an entire landlord/tenant relationship. The same goes for the snowblower you provide for tenant snow removal. For this reason, it's best to remove the equipment, make arrangements for these tasks to be done professionally, and build the cost into the rent.

You may be tempted to leave behind removable household equipment like window air conditioners. Remember if they break, you will be responsible for replacing them. Do you really want to buy a new air conditioner for a house you're going to sell? And if you are unlucky enough to get a tenant who has other plans for your property, you may find them gone altogether. However, if you live in a warm climate and the house doesn't have central air conditioning, renting it with your window air conditioners in place may be your best choice.

If you decide to leave any equipment for the tenant's use, most likely you'll have to assume responsibility for repairs, maintenance, and replacement.

Termination of Lease

Termination means ending the lease before its expiration date. You can and should put a clause in the lease that states that the lease can be terminated by the landlord for any violation of the terms of the lease. More important, include a clause that allows you to terminate the lease for no reason at all. This will give you the flexibility you need. Keep in mind that your goal is to sell the house quickly so you want to avoid issues that might delay or prevent the sale. The tenant may want the same right to terminate. If either of you can terminate the lease on one month's notice, you've created a month-to-month tenancy. The lease is still valuable since it sets forth the rest of the terms and conditions of the rental.

The termination-on-sale clause described earlier may be sufficient to at least deliver a vacant house to the new buyer. But suppose you discover that buyers are put off by the fact that there are tenants in the house. Or suppose you simply picked the wrong tenants. They don't violate the terms of the lease so they cannot be evicted for cause, but perhaps they are not the neatest people in the world. In a difficult sales market, simple things can work against the sale of the house when potential buyers view the property. Having a clause that allows you to break the lease for no cause will give you control over that situation.

If you include a clause allowing you to terminate the lease for no cause, build in reasonable notice of at least thirty days if not sixty days. Consult with an attorney and check state law since some states have a minimum time frame for notice of lease termination.

Signing the Lease

Without getting into all the specific legal issues involved in signing the lease, the following procedure is recommended:

1. The landlord sends two unsigned copies of the leases to the tenant.
2. All of the adult occupants who are leasing the house sign the lease.
3. The lease is returned to the landlord with money. This initial payment will be discussed in the next section.
4. The landlord signs the leases and returns one copy to the tenant.

In case you're wondering, by sending the lease copies unsigned you are not yet officially making an offer. If, in the interim, something comes up—say, you get a buyer or change your mind—you generally will have no obligation to go through with the deal. By obtaining the signatures of each adult renting the house, including a husband and a wife, in theory you make them each responsible for the lease. This is only in theory because first, it may not be worthwhile or practical to try to hold one party responsible for a lease that multiple parties have signed. Second, if it comes to a court action, you simply never know how these things will be enforced.

Security Deposits

It is typical to require a tenant to provide a security deposit when signing the lease. The amount is usually some multiple of the monthly rent—one or two months, for example. Some states have limits on the amount of security a landlord can require. You'll have to understand and comply with any applicable regulations that require you to maintain the security deposit in a separate interest-bearing account and pay back the deposit with some or all interest at the end of the lease term. Security deposits also will be discussed later in the section on fair housing.

It is normal to require the first month's rent with the signed lease. Some landlords also require the last month's rent as distinct from the security deposit. Obtaining the last month's rent will compensate you for the tenant who moves out without notice or without paying the rent during the last month of the lease. In theory, the landlord could simply keep the security deposit in such a case, but legal technicalities may make that difficult should the tenant wish to get back the security deposit.

Note that if you require two months' security and the first and last month's rent and the monthly rent is $1,000, your tenant will have to come up with $4,000. This can be a burden for some people, but it also indicates a certain amount of financial solvency on the part of the tenant.

It is a good idea to require initial payments in the form of a cashier's or certified bank check. You do not want a brand-new tenant who has bounced his first rent payment and the security deposit.

It is generally a violation of fair housing laws to require different security deposits. For example, you cannot charge a family with children two months' security deposit, but a couple with no children one month because you feel the children will cause more wear and tear to the house.

Returning the Deposit

Check your state laws for anything specific about the timing of returning deposits.

When the lease ends, do a complete inspection of the house and property, make a note of any damage, and get estimates for repair.

These can be deducted from the security deposit with an explanation provided to the tenant. Security deposits are designed to compensate for damage, not normal wear and tear or normal cleaning.

When Is the Rent Due?

In some states if the lease is silent about when rent payments are due, the rent is due in arrears, at the end of the month rather than at the beginning. The practice of paying the rent in advance, that is, at the beginning of the month, is so common that most people do not realize that the law may say something different. The lease can state that the rent payment is due on or before the first day of the month for which that rent payment is due.

Put in a penalty clause in the event of late payment. For example, any rent payment received after the fifth of the month will have a penalty of 5 percent or some dollar amount added to it. This penalty clause should be strictly enforced, at least in the beginning of the arrangement. Establish early on that you are serious about the rent payment date and that this whole arrangement is a business and will be conducted that way. However, if your tenant has faithfully paid the rent on time for eight months and is one day late with the payment, it is entirely up to you if you want to waive the penalty.

Use of the Premises

The house will be used for residential purposes only. You should not permit business use, home occupations, retail uses, or anything that is not a typical residential use.

There are several issues here. First, you do not want the wear and tear on your house of a business, especially one that has customers or clients coming in and out. Second, you don't want a business to damage or detract from the property. A psychologist seeing patients at the house might be one thing but an auto mechanic who has a part-time repair business in your driveway is another. Third, it may be illegal or require special permits to operate a home business in your neighborhood. And fourth, you want your house to show as a house—so even if permitted by law, you don't want a business sign on your property.

As a practical matter, having the "residential use only" provision in the lease and enforcing it may be two different things. Say your tenant runs an Internet business or is a writer, has no customers coming in and out of the house, creates no noise or other nuisance associated with the work, and puts no sign up on the property. Unless she tells you, you may not even know that there is business activity going on in the house. Note that legal restrictions may still apply. However, if houses in your area can be used for nonresidential purposes such as home occupations, you can tell prospective buyers that to enhance the appeal of the property.

Alterations and Modifications

The lease should state that tenants cannot make any alterations or modifications to the house or the property. The exception would be reasonable changes made to accommodate a handicapped tenant, which will be discussed further in the chapter on fair housing.

Use of Grounds and Accessory Buildings

It might seem obvious that a house rental would come with full use of the house, grounds, and accessory buildings (i.e., the yard, garage, storage buildings, and basement, pools, stables, etc.). Accessory building is the technical term for a detached garage or storage building. But you may want to consider some limits.

The reasons for not permitting tenant use of certain facilities or buildings on your property fall into a few common categories described here.

Liability

Use of some facilities on the property such as a swimming pool could result in your being liable if someone is injured or killed. Check with your attorney and insurance company about this.

Misuse and damage

You may have a fully equipped workshop in an outbuilding that you haven't moved yet. You will want to prevent damage to your equipment and tools and prevent injury to the tenant by prohibiting use of that particular building.

Extraordinary maintenance issues

A stable or greenhouse, for example, requires an extra amount of maintenance to keep them clean and orderly. If you're going to allow the tenants to use such buildings, it's necessary to make clear the conditions for their use and ultimately returning them in clean condition.

You need the space

You may need the space to store your furniture. If your new living arrangements are such that you can't bring all of your furniture or other possessions with you, you may want to store them in a garage or a basement. Since the expectation of most house rentals is full use of the house and grounds, you'll have to include a clause that states what the tenant is renting and specifically what is not included. In the case of a basement or garage loft, you may have to allow some tenant access while taking steps to secure your belongings.

Provision for Your Use

This is a separate issue from the previous section because it deals with your active use of the property rather than restrictions on tenant use. The part-time auto mechanic has been used previously as an example of a less-than-desirable tenant. Suppose you are the part-time mechanic and you want to continue to use your garage for your weekend work while you rent the house and live somewhere else. Depending on the physical arrangements of the property, this can be quite an intrusion on the tenants. There's a big difference if you do your work in an attached garage versus an outbuilding 500 yards away on a four-acre property.

But regardless of the physical layout, if you need to keep working a home-based business out of your property in order to maintain your income, you'll have to provide for that in the lease. You may want to offer some limits on your use, no use before or after certain times or on Sundays, for example. You may also have to address the issue of reimbursement for utility use.

Remember that you can negotiate anything, but there is a price. This type of arrangement could make the property more difficult to lease, but if you need to do this, make very clear in the preliminary negotiations that the tenants must accept this as part of the lease terms. Once the conditions are agreed to, make sure you abide by them.

Privacy / Quiet Enjoyment

There is a stipulation in most written leases and a commonly accepted unwritten guarantee in any lease that the tenant will be guaranteed "quiet enjoyment" of the premises. Don't get nervous. This does not mean that you guarantee that the neighbors won't play their TV loud after eleven o'clock.

Quiet enjoyment is simply legalese for the right of the tenant to use the premises exclusively with no interference from you or anyone else. In effect, you maintain ownership under a lease but you give up the right of possession or use of the property. Generally you have the right to enter without permission if there is an emergency. Reasonable access with notice by the landlord for such things as repairs is usually assured as part of quiet enjoyment. (You should refer to the section on owner use of the property if you are not prepared to turn over the entire premises to the tenant, and need to store some belongings in the basement, for example.)

Showing the House for Sale

The issue of quiet enjoyment discussed in the previous section takes on particular significance if you are going to continue marketing your house while you rent it. Just to be clear on this: if you decide to take your house off the market and wait for things to improve, this

51

is not an issue. If, however, you are going to actively continue to market the property while you are renting it, you'll need to be able to show the house to prospective buyers. Discuss access arrangements with the tenant and insert a clause in the lease including time of day, days of the week, and time required for advance notice. Also specify whether the buyer will be escorted or unescorted and if the tenant needs to be present.

A LEASE PROVISION FOR SHOWING THE HOUSE MIGHT READ:

Tenant agrees to permit the owner or his/her representative to escort prospective buyers or agents through the house and grounds any time between 9 A.M. and 5 P.M. on any day (Sunday through Saturday). Tenant agrees to permit such access even if tenant is not on the premises. Landlord agrees to provide tenant with at least twenty-four hours' notice of the need for access to the property and further agrees that all such inspections will be done in the presence of the owner or his/her agent.

This provision is not meant to suggest legal language but simply show how issues might be resolved.

Note the limitation on time of day, access on any day of the week, and unaccompanied visits by prospective buyers. The tenant may want to limit the hours or days for access. Do try to hold out for weekend access to the property; most buyers want to look at houses on Saturday and Sunday rather than weekdays. If you're trying to sell the house yourself, you will have to be available to escort the prospective buyers. Another provision in the lease is that the tenant is not to permit prospective buyers to inspect the house or the grounds unescorted by either the owner or the owner's agent.

As a practical matter, you'd never want the prospective buyer to visit the house unescorted. This will reduce your liability and also preclude the likelihood of the tenant saying anything negative about the property. In your conversations with the tenant, encourage them to contact you if a buyer should come back to the property after they've inspected it. Tell tenants that for their safety, they should not permit the buyer to come into the house or inspect the grounds unescorted. Finally, even if you do not plan on marketing the house while it is being rented, you may change your mind at a later date. Therefore, you may want to include these provisions just in case.

For Sale Sign

Provided local ordinances or restrictions (more about this later) do not prohibit it, it is your right to put a For Sale by Owner sign on the property or permit your real estate agent who is marketing the property to do so. The sign should indicate the phone number to call. Advise the tenant not to allow anyone to view the house who has simply stopped by in response to the sign. It is dangerous for the tenant and does not serve your interests. Prospective buyers should be directed to call the number on the sign.

Pets

This one is up to you but the wise landlord will not permit the tenant to have anything besides tropical fish. Pets can smell and cause damage. They can also be a nuisance when showing a house especially if the owner is not at home. Remember that not everyone is as fastidious about their pets as you are.

Smoking

The problem with smoking has been discussed earlier. You should try and obtain a tenant who does not smoke even if you do. Admittedly a no-smoking provision will be hard to enforce especially with guests of the tenant. But you have the right to ask the question and set the rules when interviewing prospective tenants and use it as a criterion in tenant selection.

Business Activities

This subject has also been mentioned earlier in the tenant selection criteria. It is appropriate to put a clause in the lease prohibiting any business or commercial activities from being conducted in the house or on the property. You can modify this for the right tenant if the business will involve no additional traffic, customers, or clients coming to the house, and if there is no visible evidence of business activity such as a sign on the property. Be sure and check local ordinances so that you are in compliance.

Cleaning Deposit

Consider asking the tenants for a cleaning deposit. You'll have to deliver the house in "broom clean" condition to the buyer and you want to avoid a delay in the closing or having to clean it yourself. Assuming you rent the house vacant in broom-clean condition, you can ask that the house be left in the same condition when the tenant vacates the premises. The cleaning deposit would be used only if the house were not left in the same condition as when you rented it. This deposit would be distinct from and in a different amount than the security deposit, which would be used to deal with any damage by the tenant.

Naming the Occupants

Although all the adults who are renting from you will sign the lease, it may be a good idea to name the tenants, including any children, and specifically limit occupancy to those people named. You can also add a phrase such as "and any other natural or adopted children of Mr. and Mrs. So and So" to account for any future additions to the family. This will prevent an additional family member or other people you didn't expect from moving in.

The law in some jurisdictions permits one unrelated person and their dependent children to move in without the landlord's permission. So if you rented the house to a single man and his girlfriend and her two children later moved in, in some areas you could not prevent this regardless of what the lease said.

This may seem overly cautious, but think about your own situation especially if you are moving in with family temporarily. You can always grant permission to allow additional tenants if the circumstances warrant and you feel it will not result in too much wear and tear on the house. But you don't want the tenants believing they can simply open the house up to whomever they want just because there's some extra space available.

Subleasing and Assignment

Subleasing allows the tenant to lease out the house to someone else and collect rent and pay you. Assignment allows the tenant to have someone else take over the lease and be the new tenant. Leases typically deal with these issues in some fashion, often allowing subleasing and assignment with the landlord's permission. Your lease should prohibit subletting of the property or assignment of the lease to prevent your losing control over your property.

CHAPTER FOUR ACTION POINTS

☐ Obtain copies of standardized lease forms from legal form suppliers specifically for house rentals.

☐ Review the provisions of the form with the items in this chapter to see what modifications or special provisions need to be included.

☐ Consult an attorney either to make modifications on the standard form or to write an original lease.

☐ Discuss all significant lease provisions when entering negotiations with a prospective tenant.

☐ Determine whether or not you are going to market the house while it is being rented and include lease provisions accordingly.

☐ Any decisions you make with respect to the lease should be geared toward making it easier to sell the property.

TENANT RELATIONS

BECAUSE THE SUBJECT of tenant relations is closely linked to initial negotiations and lease signing, it's included here, following the discussion of leases. This section assumes that you are going to manage the property yourself as landlord. Otherwise, property managers will deal with all these issues.

Contact Information

Give the tenants your home, business (if appropriate), and cell phone numbers as well as e-mail addresses of you and your spouse. Obtain the same information from them. Let them know the best time to call you with questions or routine matters. But make sure they understand that they should call you anytime, night or day, seven days a week, if there's an emergency.

Responding to Calls

Assuming the tenant can't reach you immediately and leaves a message, respond as soon as possible. Unless there's a detailed message, you won't know what has happened; it could be an emergency. Someone may want to see the house or a real estate agent may want to show the house without an appointment. Whatever the case, you'll want to know immediately and take whatever action is necessary.

If the tenant leaves a message that is not an emergency, return the call within twenty-four hours to show that you care about the property and the tenant, and that you respect the tenant as the other party to your business arrangement.

Complaints and Requests

The complaints and requests that a landlord will receive from a tenant can be broadly categorized as follows:

Requests that you can and should do something about—A leaky faucet, a broken furnace, and a defective appliance are examples of things that the tenant has a right to expect you to fix unless you've made other provisions in the lease. Take care of them as soon as possible.

Requests and complaints that you can do nothing about—The noisy neighbor's kids; the heat of the house in summer; or the higher-than-expected utility bills are things that you can't do anything about. Handle these complaints with diplomacy and tact, but be firm in explaining to the tenant that there is nothing you can do about them.

Try to be responsive and creative if possible. For example, if the complaint is about high heating bills, offer to have the furnace checked and cleaned. If the complaint is about noise next door, suggest that they speak to the neighbors. The idea is to not dismiss the complaint with "I can't help you."

Requests that you shouldn't do anything about—These fall into the category of favors, which were discussed earlier in the book. Using the backyard for a wedding; opening up the pool; and having the tenants' family who's moving here from Europe or South America or Mars stay in the house until they get settled are all requests you probably want to turn down. There may be circumstances where you'd be inclined to say yes, but don't. The wedding might be the exception, but only if you are assured after reviewing their plans that there will be no damage to the property or house, that there will be no neighbor complaints, and that the tenants clearly understand that this is a one-time event.

Move the Tenants In

Try to be present on the day the tenants move in. This will show them you are concerned about your property and will help prevent property damage. It would also be a good idea to schedule a walk-through with the tenant the day before they move in, before there is any furniture in the house, unless you're renting the house furnished.

Bring a movie camera or at least a still-photo camera to the walk-through and take pictures of each room. This is for the tenant's protection as well as yours so that at the end of the lease term there will be no question about the condition of the property when it was first rented.

Don't make a nuisance of yourself on moving day. You don't have to stay for the whole event but do stay for the large items of furniture to be moved in. These can damage the walls and the trim around doorways. If any damage does occur, point it out to the tenant. They've hired the movers. Be clear in indicating your expectation that the damage will be repaired by either the tenant or the moving company. Make a note of what and where the damage is. Take photos if possible.

Move the Tenants Out

You should be there on the day the tenant is moving out. In this case, you either want to stay for the entire event or be there when the last of the tenant's possessions are moved out. The idea is for you and the tenant to do a final inspection together and determine if there is any damage that warrants your keeping any portion of the security deposit.

Your lease should stipulate that the house is left broom-clean on the day the tenants move out. However, the tenants may have gotten a late start on moving day or have a great deal of furniture and other possessions or may be doing the move themselves with friends. In any case, the tenants may wish to return the next day to clean the house or several days later if they have time on the lease. Under ideal circumstances, this would all happen on moving day.

One of the reasons to obtain one or two months' security, the first and last month's rent, and/or a cleaning deposit is the possibility that the tenants will not do a final cleaning. Sometimes tenants will also not pay their last month's rent and tell you to apply the security deposit to it. If you only have one month's security and they have damaged the premises and not cleaned it, you will have lost money with the cost of repairs and cleaning.

If all goes well and the tenants leave the house pretty much the way they found it or you've agreed to the cost of any repairs that need to be done, you can return all or the balance of their security deposit within a short time of their vacating the house. State laws vary from as little as fourteen days to generally not more than thirty days.

tip

WHO'S TO BLAME?

Alice and Bill rented out their house. Unfortunately they could not be there on the day the tenants moved in. Shortly after that, Bill happened to stop by the house. He noted some gouges in the front door and on the molding around the door. He also saw several indentations in the plasterboard walls of the hallway. None of these were there when he inspected the house before renting it.

"It looks like the movers have a few repairs to do," Bill said to the tenants, trying to keep the issue as light as possible.

"Oh, that was like that when we moved in," said the tenants.

Whose fault is this? Bill and the tenant are both to blame.

Evictions

Tenants can generally be evicted for cause if they break any of the provisions of the lease, do not pay their rent, damage the premises, or break the law. They can also be evicted for not obeying a lawful order to vacate the premises, which might occur if a termination-on-sale clause is invoked. If tenants violate the terms of the lease or do not pay their rent, send a letter advising them of the violation and requesting that they either pay the rent, if that's the issue, or cease violating the lease term. The letter should be sent registered with a return receipt requested and you should keep a copy. Consult an attorney before actually threatening eviction.

In these cases, there may have been a misunderstanding of some term of the lease. Temporary financial difficulty may have delayed the rent payment. Although eviction is a last resort, you should proceed from the first communication with the idea that eviction may become necessary. Keep records of all contact with the tenants, whether through letters, e-mails, or conversations. An attorney will advise you when it is appropriate to threaten eviction and when proceedings can begin. It is preferable, however, to resolve a problem with an otherwise good tenant, rather than evict them and have to begin the rental process all over again.

Be aware that the time necessary to evict someone is different in various jurisdictions throughout the country. Judges who may be sympathetic to tenants also vary by jurisdiction.

Collect the Rent

A professional property manager sets up a rent collection system when managing one or more buildings. These systems can take the form of coupon books, monthly statements, or electronic payment. You need not develop anything elaborate, but you do need to think about how you are going to collect the monthly rent.

It is simplest to have the tenant send you a check or money order by mail each month. If you want to make life even easier for the tenant, you can provide twelve self-addressed unstamped envelopes for the tenant's use. The tenant's canceled check will serve as a receipt of payment.

Alternatively, you can arrange to personally pick up the rent each month if you are living in the area. This procedure has the advantage of allowing you an opportunity to routinely inspect the property and make sure it's being well cared for. It also sends a signal to the tenant that you are not an absentee landlord, and that you intend to keep a watchful eye on the property. If you do collect the rent personally, have a receipt book with you for that tenant who might want to pay the rent in cash. These books are generally available at stationery and legal document supply stores.

You may feel uncomfortable collecting the rent personally every month. Even if you have what it takes to be a landlord, you may not be comfortable dealing with the tenant unless you have to. You may also feel that a monthly visit is an intrusion. It's not. But for whatever reason, if you can't or don't want to collect the rent personally, you must establish the procedure for rent payment at the beginning of the tenancy. One simple method is to provide the tenant with twelve addressed envelopes, that they can use to mail the rent check. If it is acceptable to them, you could also make arrangements with their bank and yours for automatic payment each month from their account.

Late Fees

You have built into the lease a provision for a penalty if the rent is paid late. This penalty is generally either a flat dollar amount or a small percentage of the lease. Do not view the late payment penalty as a way to make extra money by charging an exorbitant amount and hoping the tenant pays late. The late payment penalty should be an inducement to the tenant to pay on time.

When do you charge the late payment penalty? Stated another way, do you wish to give the tenant a grace period in which to pay the rent? If, for example, the rent is due on the first of the month, a late payment penalty may be assessed if the rent is paid after the third of the month. This should all be spelled out in the lease, of course. Be aware that a grace period often becomes the due date for the rent. If the rent is due on the first of the month and no penalty is charged until after the third, tenants will often mail the check to you on the first rather than a few days before.

Some states have restrictions on the amount you can charge for a late penalty payment. In general, if you keep the late payment penalty within a maximum of 4 percent of the rent, you should be okay, but check with state or local authorities about this. The easiest thing to do is to add on a rounded flat-fee penalty based on the maximum percentage allowable. See the chapter on real estate math for an example of this.

Be cautious in waiving the late payment penalty. A regularly paying tenant who's been in the house for the better part of a year may deserve to have the late payment penalty waived. A tenant whose second month's rent payment is late may equally deserve the break but probably shouldn't get it since you have no way to evaluate whether late payments will become a pattern. You do have the advantage of only having one tenant so you can be as flexible in this as you like.

Nonpayment of Rent

If a tenant is late beyond the grace period, advise them of the rent due and the late payment fees. If you wish, you can provide them with a Pay Rent or Quit notice, which in effect is the first step in the eviction process. A Pay Rent or Quit notice generally takes the form of a letter to the tenant advising them that they have so many days (usually as few as five to seven) to pay all back and current rent or to vacate the premises or be subject to eviction. Models of this form may be found in the reference books and websites noted in the reference section of this book. As with any legal document, particularly one that may result in an eviction action, you may want to consult an attorney before sending out a Pay Rent or Quit Notice.

Different states and communities have varying rules regarding when the notice may be given to the tenant and how long after that eviction proceedings may be begun. If a straightforward conversation with the tenant does not result in full payment of the rent with the late payment penalty, consult local or state authorities or your attorney as to how to proceed.

Since this is one of those confrontational subjects we'd all rather avoid, your tendency will be to ignore this whole issue and hope it never comes up. You may, however, wish to do a little research and familiarize yourself with the eviction proceedings at the beginning of your landlording experience. In the event it becomes necessary to evict someone, you will then have all the information at hand.

Don't Break the Law

Under no circumstances should you resort to direct physical confrontation or removal of a tenant's possessions from the house as a way to evict them. The stories you may have heard about a landlord's throwing the tenant's furniture and clothing onto the sidewalk and changing the locks on the property are highly exaggerated. And where true, have probably resulted in court action against the landlord. Rules will vary by jurisdiction and sometimes by property type. Judges in areas where there are a great many tenants are often sympathetic to the tenant's plight. You may get a break because you are not a professional landlord/investor but are simply renting out your own home for a period of time. Or you may have to wait because a sympathetic judge doesn't want to throw a family out during the holidays.

Whatever the case and whatever your personal feelings about your rights as a property owner, due process for eviction must be followed. The best thing you can do is consult the law and/or an attorney before taking any steps that will ultimately lead to an involuntary removal of the tenant.

CHAPTER FIVE ACTION POINTS

☐ Tenant relations are not about being social with the tenant but are about managing the property to your benefit as the owner while fulfilling your obligations as the landlord.

☐ Provide tenants with appropriate information to allow them to contact you at any time and respond promptly to all calls and complaints.

☐ Be present on the day the tenant moves in and moves out.

☐ Take photographs or video of the house when the tenant moves in.

☐ Prepare a checklist of items to look at so you won't forget anything on moving-out day.

☐ Decide how you're going to collect the rent.

☐ Decide about grace periods and late penalty fees.

☐ Think carefully before you waive a late payment fee.

☐ Grant one-time favors sparingly if at all.

☐ Research eviction proceedings, just in case.

CHAPTER SIX

FAIR HOUSING LAWS

YOU ARE GOING to rent one house; you hope once. You do not need to become an expert in fair housing and anti-housing discrimination law. On the other hand, you don't want your one experience as a landlord to result in being on the wrong end of a lawsuit and paying a hefty fine.

Understanding and following the premise that only monetary discrimination in housing is acceptable will help keep you out of trouble. All other things being equal, if a tenant has the ability to pay the rent and fulfill the other obligations of the lease, she should be permitted to rent. The details of fair housing laws, however, can be complex and are worth elaboration.

Federal, State, and Local Laws

Modern fair housing laws date to 1968 with subsequent amendments. State and local fair housing laws have been passed to supplement the federal law. It's important to understand this relationship among the three levels of laws.

Everyone is subject to all federal fair housing laws. Owners of property of a particular state are subject to the federal fair housing laws plus their individual state fair housing laws. And finally residents of a municipality are subject to all three levels of law.

Through the years many states and municipalities have passed laws to supplement the federal fair housing laws. In all cases state and municipal provisions are stricter than the federal law. This means that while the federal law may not protect a certain group of people or may provide for an exception to the law, a state law may protect that group or may have removed the exception.

Federal fair housing laws are discussed here. Check your state and local laws to determine how they may affect your decisions regarding tenant selection. For informational purposes only, examples of the groups not protected under fair housing laws will be provided and exceptions to the law explained. In no way should this be interpreted as condoning any form of discrimination, legal or otherwise.

What You Can't Do

Certain acts in the rental of housing are prohibited under federal law. You should note that these prohibited acts apply only to certain groups or what are called "protected classes," which we'll discuss in the next section. Prohibited activities include:

Refusing to rent

You cannot refuse to rent to people if they are members of a protected class.

Changing the terms and conditions

You cannot, for example, charge one person one month's security and another person two months' security simply because they are members of a protected class. The same applies to different rental amounts or the length of the lease.

Discriminatory statements or advertising

You may not use any discriminatory advertising or statements in renting the house. There are many obviously discriminatory statements and you would most likely have a difficult time finding a reputable newspaper to publish them. There are subtler statements also that you should avoid. For example, gender is a protected class and it could be considered discriminatory to advertise a house with a "woman's dream kitchen" or a "man's dream garage workshop." When advertising your house for rent (and for sale), it is best to stick to a physical description of the property.

Using false or questionable statements as a means of discrimination

This again is a subtler means by which to discriminate. For example, it would be discriminatory if you talked about the poor quality of the local schools to a family with children because you didn't want to rent to them, when the local schools were actually highly rated.

Even statements that are factually true can have a discriminatory effect. For example, you know that your current tenant is definitely moving in a month and you tell a prospective tenant that the house is not available because it is currently rented. This statement is factually true; however, it possibly can be construed as a means of discrimination if the prospective tenant is a member of a protected class.

Protected Classes

Protected class is the term used to describe a characteristic against which you may not discriminate. The protected classes under federal law are as follows:

Race and color

A particular aspect of federal fair housing law is that none of the exceptions apply where race or color is concerned.

National origin

Essentially this refers to the country where a person was born or where his or her ancestors were born. It does not mean the country of current citizenship. Under federal law, it is acceptable to discriminate in a rental situation against someone who is not an American citizen. However, as with any legally permitted discrimination, it must be applied consistently. So if you choose not to rent to a citizen of Country A you must also not rent to a citizen of Country B or C. Or else it might be viewed as discrimination on the basis of national origin and not citizenship.

Sex (gender)

This prohibition applies to discriminating on the basis of gender, but does not refer to sexual orientation. It is legal under federal fair housing law to discriminate against homosexuals.

Handicap

Handicapped persons must be allowed to make reasonable modifications at their own expense to the rental unit. They must also agree to remove the modifications and restore the premises to their original condition when they leave. In all likelihood, this may not be an issue for you in renting your house. You are seeking a relatively short-term rental and most people will be reluctant to spend any substantial sum of money to modify a place they won't be staying in very long.

Reasonable modifications are things like installing grab bars in the shower. Lowering all the kitchen counters or installing an elaborate ramp outside the house would most likely not be considered reasonable under the circumstances of your rental. Understand that these decisions are subject to interpretation by local equal rights commissions and the courts and may differ from your opinion.

Note that assistive animals such as seeing-eye dogs are generally held to be exempt from rules against pets under the idea that a landlord also must make reasonable accommodations for the handicapped.

Familial status

Confusion here often stems from a misunderstanding of the term. Familial status is not the same as marital status. Familial status refers to the presence of children in the family. Therefore you may not refuse to rent to someone simply because you don't want children in the house.

It should be noted that nothing in this part of the law requires you to rent to a family whose number of people including children would violate health and building codes as to occupancy. The general rule of thumb is two people per bedroom so a maximum of six people in a three-bedroom house. That number should be verified with your local building and/or health department.

State and Local Laws

States and municipalities have supplemented federal fair housing laws by adding protected classes to the federal list. In some cases, municipalities have added protected classes that have not been added by the state. Therefore it is possible that a group is protected in one city within a state but not in the rest of the state. Some of the protected classes that have been added by states and municipalities are as follows:

Age

Age discrimination generally covers people over eighteen years of age. It may also cover so-called emancipated minors in your area.

Citizenship status

Citizenship status as has been mentioned refers to whether or not the individual is a citizen of the United States. In some jurisdictions, it is also discriminatory to refuse to rent to an illegal alien.

Handicapping conditions

Handicapping conditions have been further defined by some jurisdictions to include learning disabilities and mental handicapping conditions so as to expand the definition beyond the typical physical handicap that we are familiar with.

Lawful occupation

Lawful occupation as a protected class refers to the practice of refusing to rent to an individual because we don't like his or her job. Lawful occupation means that the occupation must be legal, so we do not have to rent to a known drug dealer, but we cannot refuse to rent to an attorney because we fear we might be sued.

Lawful source of income

Lawful source of income refers to the fact that in some areas one may not discriminate against renters whose sole source of income is social security or public assistance or other legal source.

Marital status

Marital status as a protected class prohibits discrimination on the basis of whether two people are married or not.

Military status

Military status prohibits discrimination on the basis of whether or not the tenant is a member of the active or reserve components of the military. In case you're wondering why some jurisdictions have added this as a protected class, there are owners who would discriminate on this basis because of the uncertainty of the time frame someone in the military might be in the area. Furthermore, there are generally laws that allow people called to active military duty to sometimes be able to break a lease without further obligation.

Sexual orientation

Sexual orientation is not a protected class under federal law. It is, however, a protected class in several states and municipalities, so check with your local human rights or equal opportunity agency if this is an issue for you. Note that while your state may be one that has adopted laws prohibiting same-sex marriage, sexual orientation may still be a protected class.

Exceptions

There are a number of very specific exceptions to the federal fair housing law. The one most applicable to our discussion in this section permits the owner of one single-family home to discriminate in the rental of that home under certain conditions. The exemption does not apply to the investor who owns four or more homes and rents them out.

You must meet two conditions to take advantage of this exemption. First, you may not advertise the property. Second, you may not use a real estate agent to help you rent the property. It should be noted that the exemption is not available when used on the basis of race or color, even if the stated conditions are met.

Although we're mostly discussing the rental of single-family homes in this book, you may be in a situation where you own a two-family (duplex, two flat) house and you live in one apartment and rent the other. Now you have to move and temporarily wish to rent the other apartment while you wait to sell the house. The exemption is only available in two-family houses (duplexes) if they are owner occupied.

Before you avail yourself of an exception, you should also check your state and local laws. One of the ways states and municipalities have strengthened fair housing laws in their own jurisdictions has been to remove or modify the federal exceptions in some way.

Role of the Real Estate Agent

Real estate agents are prohibited by law from engaging in discriminatory housing practices. You, of course, should not be attempting to engage in illegal discrimination in the rental of your house. You should not ask a real estate agent to assist you in illegally discriminating. As noted in the section on exemptions, even if you are able to qualify for an exception, a real estate agent may not assist you even if the exception itself is legal.

Discriminatory Deed Restrictions

A deed restriction or covenant is a statement placed in a deed by a previous owner that prohibits or requires certain actions on the part of all future owners of that property. Restrictions usually relate to the use or physical nature of the property or home. A typical restriction might require the homeowner to paint his or her house one of five prescribed colors or to build all additions to the house in keeping with a certain style of architecture.

In many parts of the country, it was common to place restrictions in the deed that prohibited the sale or rental of the property to people of certain religious, ethnic, or racial groups. With the passage of federal fair housing laws where for the most part the groups mentioned in these deed restrictions are members of protected classes, these restrictions became void and carry no legal weight. In fact, due to the passage of fair housing laws, it would be illegal to obey these deed restrictions.

Avoiding Discrimination Complaints

I'm going on the assumption here that you will avoid any purposeful discrimination in renting your house. I'm assuming that the concern is an unintentional breach of fair housing laws or a misunderstanding of some kind on the part of the tenant who may feel that you've discriminated against them. Here are a few things you can do minimize your risk.

- Avoid discriminatory behavior even if no discrimination is intended.
- Set your mind that you are going to rent to the most financially qualified tenant who meets the other legally acceptable criteria you have set for tenant selection.
- Check state and local laws that may apply to protected classes and exceptions.
- Be conscious of treating all prospective tenants the same way. A cup of coffee offered to one should be offered to all.
- Keep accurate records of applicants, conversations, lease terms.
- Avoid discriminatory questions. For example in an area where marital status is a protected class, "Are you married?" is considered a discriminatory question to ask a couple.

CHAPTER SIX ACTION POINTS

☐ Become familiar with fair housing laws at the federal, state, and local levels.

☐ Be aware there are exceptions to the federal fair housing laws that may apply to your situation of renting your house.

☐ Note that there are no exceptions to anyone with respect to race and color.

☐ The best way to avoid a fair housing complaint is to avoid discrimination and discriminatory behavior in renting the house.

☐ Treat every prospective tenant the same.

☐ Avoid discriminatory comments, questions, and advertising.

☐ Keep good records.

☐ Discriminate only on the basis of financial condition.

ZONING CODES AND OTHER RESTRICTIONS

THERE ARE VERY few federal laws that govern the physical issues associated with the use of properties or buildings. Historically, states, counties, and local municipalities enact and enforce these laws and regulations. You'll have to do your homework and research the specifics at your local municipal building. Remember that municipality may mean a county, city, town, village, township, or borough.

Zoning Ordinances and Legal Requirements

Most municipalities have a zoning ordinance in place to govern land use. While a zoning ordinance can be very complex, for our purposes, it governs what you can build on your property and what you can do with it. It does this by dividing the municipality into zones or districts with specific uses permitted in each district.

For example, a municipality will likely have one or more districts where single-family houses may be built and other districts where commercial uses are permitted. It is highly unlikely that there is a zoning ordinance that prohibits the rental of an otherwise legally built home. Problems occur when the use itself may be illegal, or the homeowner tries to skirt the law.

Specifically, if you plan to rent your house to a tenant who is going to use part of the house for a home-based business, you'll need to check that this is legal. As a practical matter, if there is no external evidence of the business operation—no customers, no traffic, no sign, and no noise—it would be difficult for the authorities to ascertain that a business is being conducted in the house. But technically it may be a violation of the zoning ordinance. The zoning ordinance may also control things such as parking commercial vehicles outside overnight or storage of boats or recreational vehicles on the property.

Zoning also controls the number of dwelling units on a particular piece of property. Suppose your house is located in a one-family house zone. Renting an apartment in the basement is illegal. Now you're going to rent out the main part of the house while continuing to rent the basement apartment. This is also illegal and more problematic.

A disgruntled or evicted tenant may report the illegal apartment. There may be additional safety issues relative to renting out an apartment. Fines may be levied if you are caught.

Your relationship to the property and the tenant is a serious one that has some liability attached. Your safest course of action is to be sure that you are in complete compliance with all laws, including zoning laws.

Lead paint

According to federal law if your house was built before 1978, you must provide your prospective tenant a copy of a lead paint disclosure form before the lease can take effect. You must also provide a copy of the federal booklet that explains lead paint hazards.

The form itself has you acknowledge lead paint hazards; deny any knowledge of any lead paint hazards; or state that you have no knowledge of lead paint hazards. The tenants in turn have ten days in which to have the house tested. Testing is not mandatory. Should the tenants choose to have the house tested and lead paint is found, they can negotiate with you to have it removed or they can get out of the lease and have any deposit returned. They can also choose to proceed with the lease with no further action with respect to the lead paint.

If as a result of a prospective sale or lease, or for any other reason, you have already had the house tested for lead paint and it has been found, you are required to provide those reports to a prospective tenant.

As newer houses have been built and older homes renovated and repainted many times with nonlead-based paint, the incidence of inspections as well as discovery of lead-based paint has diminished. Often, unless a family has very young children who are particularly susceptible to lead poisoning, they will not bother to test or be put off by a warning that you do not know about the presence of lead-based paint. Nonetheless you are required to provide the notification if your house was built before 1978. And note that no matter how many renovations or repaintings you've done, the original lead paint may be present and you still need to provide notification and the booklet.

Mold

Mold is the most recent environmental hazard that has come to the attention of homebuyers and renters. Sensitivity to mold varies among individuals. Remediation of mold is not simply a matter of painting over it or cleaning it with bleach. Remediation should be done by a trained technician.

There is no federal requirement regarding disclosure of mold, but there may be state or municipal requirements. Disclosures can take the form of notification to a prospective tenant that they may wish to have the house tested without there being an actual notice by the owner/landlord that there is mold present.

You should check with your state real estate commission and/or local health department to determine if a mold disclosure form is required in your area. If you are using a real estate agent to sell your house, you might also ask her. Generally speaking any disclosure of an environmental hazard that is required by a seller will also most likely be required of a landlord. Read the later section on material fact disclosure where mold is discussed again.

Asbestos

Asbestos is another potential environmental hazard that may be found in your house. Asbestos is a mineral that was used for many years for fireproofing and insulation around pipes. As it became known that asbestos dust and fibers could cause serious lung ailments, it became necessary to identify, disclose, and take steps to remediate the effects of asbestos if it was present.

There is no federal law requiring disclosure or remediation of asbestos, but there may be requirements in your own state or municipality.

Radon

Radon is an odorless, colorless radioactive gas that is caused by the decay of other radioactive substances such as certain types of rocks. Once again there are no federal testing, disclosure, or remediation requirements, though there may be local laws governing disclosures regarding radon.

Physical condition and other disclosures

Many states have property disclosures that require statements by the owner to a buyer regarding the condition of the property as it is known to the owner. Generally, these do not require any testing or remediation but are merely used to provide information to the prospective buyer.

If your state or municipality requires such a disclosure, you need to determine whether you as the landlord/owner need to provide a disclosure to the prospective tenant. You should be able to research this with your state real estate commission or your real estate agent if you are using one. This type of disclosure is generally not required to be provided to tenants.

It is important to comply with all the rules regarding disclosure forms and to complete them honestly. Failure to provide the form if you're required to do so or knowingly lying on the form can result in fines as well as civil and potentially criminal liability.

Latent defects and environmental hazards

There is an entire area of real estate law that has developed through the years that has softened the traditional "buyer beware" approach that existed for many years. There may be physical issues that are present in the house that can range from an inconvenience to a hazard. A leaky roof can be annoying and eventually cause damage. Faulty electrical wiring can cause a fire. Many of these defects are not easily identified even by an inspection by a knowledgeable and trained person. They are generally referred to as hidden or latent defects.

The law varies somewhat from state to state and case to case on this subject. Even if your state does not have a mandatory property condition or hazard disclosure form, you may be required to reveal all latent defects to a prospective buyer or tenant. In some cases the disclosure may only be required in sales transactions, so as a landlord you don't need to reveal anything to your tenant beyond the mandatory federal disclosures and those that may apply in your state.

As a practical matter though, would you want to rent out a house with faulty wiring? And if you knew about the faulty wiring and didn't tell the tenant and someone was hurt in a resulting fire, would you be liable?

The same rules usually apply to environmental hazards. If you know about radon in your house and have not had it corrected, your best bet is to disclose it to your prospective tenants and let them make an informed decision about whether to rent. Better still, have the problem corrected so it won't interfere with the sale of the house later.

Building Codes

If zoning ordinances are designed to tell you what your property can be used for and what you can build on your land, building codes will tell you how you must build it. More specifically, building codes provide minimum standards for safe construction. In recent years, building codes have also addressed environmental and conservation concerns in structures.

Noncompliance with building codes can lead to serious liability issues for you as a landlord. You are required to provide a safe, habitable dwelling for your tenants. If something is not in accordance with the building code or has not been properly permitted and someone is injured as a result, you will most likely bear financial liability.

Think of it this way. If the deck you built without a building permit collapses under your feet, who are you going to sue? Yourself? But if that same deck collapses under your tenant's feet, who is the tenant going to sue? Same answer. You.

If you're sued, you'll have to prove that the deck was built in accordance with all design and safety standards in accordance with the building code and properly permitted. Your insurance company may refuse to cover the accident if it wasn't.

Get the proper permits if there is any construction on your property that either you've built or was built before you bought the house and is not properly permitted. This is something you should do anyway when selling your house.

The place to start this process is usually the municipal building department or code enforcement office.

Fire and Safety Codes

You'll need to check with the local building department or code enforcement office to determine if there are any special fire or safety regulations you need to follow if you are renting your house. These regulations are based on the theory that owner/occupants will be vigilant about their own safety, but a tenant may need protection from a less-than-diligent landlord. Even though safety and fire regulations are usually aimed at multitenant buildings, there may be rules in your municipality that apply to any rental dwelling.

You should inquire about the requirements for, location, and type of each of the following:

- Smoke detectors
- Carbon monoxide detectors
- Fire extinguishers
- Number of exits
- Emergency exits
- Exit lighting
- Height and size of windows in bedrooms
- Second-floor and above emergency escape equipment
- Emergency lighting
- Basement used as finished space (if applicable)

A number of these items may be required as safety items for you as a resident occupant anyway. Smoke and carbon monoxide detectors have become standard requirements in most municipalities. Also, this is a comprehensive list but may not be complete for your municipality. Any safety equipment that is required or that you provide voluntarily must be maintained. Do not depend on the tenant to change the batteries in the smoke detector twice a year.

 KEEP IT LEGAL

It seems a landlord had rented out a basement apartment in a one-family house. The zoning did not permit this type of rental. The authorities discovered the illegal apartment after more than a year, and the tenant was made to move. The tenant went to court and sued the landlord for renting him an illegal apartment. The court awarded the tenant all of the rent he had paid. Ouch!

A far worse consequence was reported in a newspaper article about a seller who knew about but neglected to advise his buyer of a faulty furnace. One of the members of the buyer's family died as a result of carbon monoxide poisoning. The seller went to jail for manslaughter. If you replace "seller" with "landlord" and "buyer" with "tenant," the scenario is unchanged.

To minimize your liability, if you notice any unsafe or improper use of space by the tenants, ask the tenant to stop, or remove the hazard. Many municipalities, for example, have strict requirements for use of basement space for bedroom purposes. If your basement doesn't meet those requirements and the tenant uses the basement as a bedroom, you could find yourself liable to some degree if someone is injured or killed. All such cease and desist conversations should be followed up in writing so that there is a record of the notice.

Exits and entrances

This is one subject dealing with safety issues important enough to be treated separately. All entrances and exits from your house must remain unrestricted and well lighted. That means tenants need to receive keys to that front door you've never used because you always use the side door. It means the stuff you will continue to store in the basement should not block the basement door. All outside entrances and exits should be well lighted.

Remember that how you have lived in your house has been your choice and it generally affects only you and your family. Your obligations as a landlord are different.

The furnace and water heater

This is the second safety subject that should be mentioned separately. Carbon monoxide is an odorless, colorless, and very deadly gas. It can result from incomplete or poor combustion from gas- and oil-fired furnaces and water heaters.

Make sure furnaces and water heaters have sufficient oxygen available to burn properly. If you're not sure about this, check with your plumber, heating oil company, or the building inspector. Have your furnace and water heater checked and serviced before you move a new tenant into the house. And keep a record of the service call. Make any repairs promptly that are recommended by the service company. Respond to tenant complaints immediately, especially if they involve the heating system. Unless you are a trained trades person, get the appropriate expert in right away.

The importance of maintaining a safe home-heating and water-heating system cannot be emphasized too highly. You would not want to be responsible for someone's injury or death either through willful neglect or lack of knowledge. The liability in these situations can be both financial and criminal depending on the specific circumstances.

Well water

If your house is supplied with well water as opposed to a municipal or private water company supply, have your water tested before renting. While not necessarily regulated, you should do this periodically anyway and may have to do it before selling your house.

Deed and Other Restrictions

Deed restrictions were mentioned earlier in the context of fair housing laws. Deed restrictions may be used for many other purposes. Deed restrictions or covenants are designed to control things that the zoning and building codes either can't or won't. For example, very few building codes specify the material that must be used on the outside of the house beyond some general requirements such as wood, cement or vinyl siding, stone, or brick. A deed restriction in a particular subdivision may require that all homes be sided in wood only. This of course will not impact your decision to rent the house.

But suppose there is a restriction against home businesses. We've discussed the impact that a zoning regulation may have on a tenant who wishes to operate a home business. A deed restriction also may forbid parking commercial vehicles overnight in the driveway, and your prospective tenant has to bring his company work truck home every night. There may be similar deed restrictions on boats or recreational vehicles. If such restrictions exist, this would most likely be a case where the original subdivider of the property wanted to put resections on the lots that were not covered by the zoning. Also, if a deed restriction says one thing and public law says another, the stricter rule applies. Generally, this will be the deed restriction.

There may even be a restriction on renting the house. This would be most unusual, but there are some pretty unusual deed restrictions. You need to look at your deed or have your attorney or real estate agent look at the deed to see if there are any restrictions that would somehow limit your ability to rent the property. Probably, you are completely free to rent the property, but you may have to turn down a tenant because of how he intends to use the property. A review of possible deed restrictions will also help you to ask the right questions when interviewing a prospective tenant.

Condominiums

If you own and want to rent a condominium, check what are sometimes referred to as the covenants, conditions, and restrictions. These are the rules governing the sale and use of the condominium. Much like typical single-family homes, it is unlikely that there would be a restriction on rental of the unit. However, it may be that you have to formally obtain permission from the condominium association through the board of directors in order to rent.

You will also want to check on any restrictions such as home businesses that may affect your choice of a prospective tenant. You should also be clear with the new tenants about the amenities that go with rental of the unit. In some cases, membership in the health club or use of certain facilities within the condominium complex may carry an extra fee beyond the common charges. This will be especially true in golf course communities. You'll want to make sure your tenant knows what's included in their rent.

Cooperative apartments

If you are renting a cooperative apartment, you will need to check the rules and regulations that apply. Be sure to read the appropriate documents—prospectus and cooperative rules and restrictions (house rules)—that you received when you purchased the unit, and check with the board and/or the management if you have any questions. As with the rental of any dwelling unit, you will want to inform the tenant of anything they can't do that is beyond your ability to control or grant permission for as the landlord.

If you own a cooperative, you already know that you had to obtain board approval to purchase the unit in the first place. You also know that there is great concern among all the tenant/owners about nonpayment of common charges. Consequently, it is very likely that you will have to obtain approval by the cooperative board to rent your unit. It is also possible that the board may not approve renting the unit or may want to approve the tenant before permitting you to sign the lease. It is important that you understand all rules and regulations before offering your unit for rent.

If the board will not approve the rental of your unit under any circumstances, you can put all your energies, time, and money into trying to sell the unit. If the board will permit rental of the unit but wants approval of the tenant, then you need to find out what information the board will want from the tenant in order to make their decision and request that information from the prospective tenants. You will also need to explain to them that their application will be subject to the approval of the board.

Material Facts

A material fact is defined in real estate terms as a fact (not an opinion or speculation) that most people would want to know about before making a decision whether to buy or rent a property. Disclosure of material facts is a requirement associated with the duties of a real estate agent and extends not only to what an agent knows but what he or she should have known. The question of disclosure of known material facts by a landlord to a tenant may not be quite as clear since the decision the tenant is making is not as permanent as the decision a buyer or seller is making.

However, the obvious question is, if you know something that may affect the tenant's decision to rent the house, why not tell them? Perhaps you didn't really think it would matter to the tenant, or you didn't want to lose the rental.

In the first case, put yourself in the tenant's position and err on the side of too much information. The fact that they will be redistricting the schools in your area may be of concern to a family with children. The imminent construction of the new sewage treatment plant down the street might be of interest to your prospective tenant. Neither of these things might bother you but these and other things that may be happening in the area may affect the tenant's decision. On the other hand, the fact that they are raising taxes next year would be of interest to a buyer but not to a residential tenant (commercial property tenants often have to pay taxes in addition to rent).

In the second case of not wanting to lose the tenant, you've already decided not to be completely forthcoming. If the fact has not been disclosed and is important to the tenant, you will end up with a very unhappy tenant. And the tenant may be unhappy enough to try to break the lease. And while you may have a lease that binds the tenant to the property for a period of time, do you really want to rent your house, the house you eventually want to sell, to someone who feels you were less than honest with them?

CHAPTER SEVEN ACTION POINTS

☐ Check the zoning ordinance and deed for any restrictions on the use of the property.

☐ Check the building, fire, and safety codes to make sure your house is in compliance for renting.

☐ Make corrections and repairs needed and file for the proper permits to bring your house into compliance with local laws.

☐ Prepare a checklist of safety items for regular maintenance, such as replacing batteries in smoke detectors.

☐ Check with the appropriate board or management about renting if you own a condominium or cooperative.

☐ Make sure all exits and entrances are clear and well lighted.

☐ Have the furnace and water heater serviced and tested.

☐ Research required environmental and physical condition disclosures and obtain necessary disclosure forms and materials.

☐ Disclose latent defects and material facts to prospective tenants.

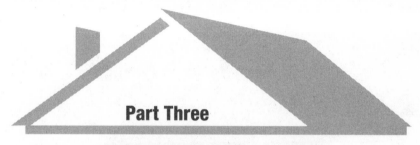

Part Three

MANAGING THE PROPERTY

CHAPTER EIGHT
BUDGETS

THE FINANCES OF your rental property should be considered as part of the decision-making process of whether to rent your house while you wait to sell it. The information in Chapter 19, "Real Estate Math," should also be consulted.

Pro Forma

A real estate investor and/or a professional property manager creates what in the business is called a pro forma to analyze a property's expenses and project a budget for operating the property. It is also called a reconstructed operating statement. The term *reconstructed* is used because it is a projection based on previous experience, namely prior expenses and income. The projection is based on a one-year annual budget but can be broken down into monthly increments. Creating a pro forma will give you a better sense of what to expect as you rent the property. This exercise will not magically make a nonprofitable property profitable, but it should help avoid any nasty financial surprises. The basic format of the pro forma, slightly modified for our purposes, is as follows:

> Potential Gross Income
> – Vacancy and Collection Loss
> = Effective Gross Income
> – Expenses (Fixed Expenses, Variable Expenses, and Reserves)
> = Net Operating Income
> – Mortgage Expenses
> = **Cash Flow**

Potential Gross Income—Set the Rent

In the classic pro forma, the potential gross income is estimated first, and the first step is to set the rent. Reasonable flexibility in arriving at the final rent will probably be your best approach.

Prospective tenants may expect a bit more flexibility in renting a single-family house in today's market than they would in renting an apartment. Perhaps they feel that with only one dwelling unit to rent, the landlord cannot be too rigid. This might especially be true since they may know you're trying to sell the property and this is only a temporary situation. Whatever the reason, don't give up your negotiating position too quickly but be prepared to respond to market conditions and a good prospective tenant.

Setting the Rent—The Wrong Way

You may be tempted to look at the expenses related to your house and set the rent accordingly. Your rent calculation will look something like this:

+ Mortgage Payment
+ Taxes
+ Maintenance
+ Utilities
= Rent

Every investor, landlord, and property manager wishes it were done that way. The fact is that for a variety of economic reasons rents often don't keep pace with the prices of properties. Remember that you bought the property originally to live in, not to rent out as an investment. You may have been willing and able to take on a high mortgage payment, but this bears no relationship to the rental value of the property.

If you bought the property years ago, you either have paid off the original mortgage or have very low payments. If you refinanced, you did so to lower your payments, although taxes, utilities, and maintenance have gone up. It is likely in this case that the current market rents will cover most or all of the costs related to the property.

In the not-so-ideal situation, you bought the house at the height of the recent market and took out an adjustable rate mortgage that has now adjusted upward. Another situation is that although you bought the house years ago, you took advantage of the rise in equity to refinance and your payments now are higher than when you bought the house.

Regardless of the scenario, renting your house while you wait to sell it may be the wisest course of action. The market will determine the rent you can charge, not your need to cover your bills.

Setting the Rent—The Right Way

The correct way to set the rent for a rental unit is to research the market for similar rentals. You may have heard the term *comparables* or *comps* from your real estate agent. A similar property with available information regarding price (if one is selling or buying) or rental rates may be a comparable.

Start your market research with the newspaper but don't ignore the free magazines you get at the supermarket or the diner. Go online to any site you can find that may list rentals in your area. Ask your real estate agent, if you are using one, to do a little research for you. An ideal comparable would have these characteristics identical to your house:

- Location—including school district
- Size—both gross size and number of bedrooms
- Curb appeal
- Quality
- Level of maintenance and upkeep
- Amenities—swimming pool, etc.
- Size of property

To qualify this house as a useful comparable, you would need to know what it actually rented for after the lease was signed. This is almost impossible unless it's a neighbor's house and the neighbor is willing to share the information. Unlike sold houses, there are neither public nor searchable real estate brokerage records of residential leases. You may be able to glean some general information from local news stories, the chamber of commerce, and the local economic development agency, if there is one. But the best you'll probably be able to do is to research houses that are currently for rent.

tip

RENT: THE REAL WORLD

In the ideal world, the rent is equal to all of the property's expenses plus a profit. In the real world, the rent is a factor of how many competing properties are available and what their rents are. Many of the failures of new real estate investors have been because they thought they lived in the ideal rather than the real world.

Don't forget to tap into the local real estate agent's knowledge. Whether or not you've actually engaged a real estate agent, you'll find that they are always looking for business and are usually willing to talk with you and answer your questions. Their hope is that when you do sell your house you'll list it with them, so don't be afraid to call an agent and ask some questions about the rental market.

Suppose you can't find houses like yours for rent. Look for large apartments in duplexes that meet the other criteria. If you can't find anything in your neighborhood, look at other neighborhoods.

Now that you've located some similar houses or apartments for rent, you're going to have to do some legwork. Make an appointment and visit as many of the houses or apartments as you can. Get a notebook to write down the important facts about the property.

At the end of the property visit, between your own observations and questions you will have asked the agent or the owner, you should have the following information in your notebook for each property:

- Address
- Neighborhood or subdivision—if it has a name
- School district

- Single family or apartment
- Approximate square footage
- Number of rooms
- Number of bedrooms
- Number of bathrooms
- Amenities
- Size of lot
- What is included in the rent
- What extra bills beyond the rent the tenant is responsible for
- Any duties associated with rental (e.g., snow removal)

The following items are less objective and will require some judgment on your part. Take a good look at your house, trying to put yourself in the eyes of a tenant. You may want your family to go through this with you. For the most part, don't bother to ask friends or extended family members. They will usually tell you what you want to hear rather than the truth.

Using a scale of Poor, Fair, Good, and Excellent, rate your house on the following criteria:

- Curb appeal
- Condition/maintenance and upkeep of the house
- Condition/maintenance and upkeep of the lot
- Quality of the kitchen—how new
- Quality of the bathrooms—how new
- Quality of the neighborhood
- Quality of the school district
- Functionality of the house—how well the floor plan works

First, be as objective as you can. We all think our houses are excellent. Try to look at it with the eyes of a prospective tenant who will pay you money to live there.

Second, don't obsess over the difference between good and excellent or fair and good. You're going to do the ratings and there are no right or wrong answers. This part of the process is just a starting place from which to make comparisons. If it's easier you can also use a one to five rating system.

The next step is to evaluate every comparable you see on the same items. The only difference is that instead of the scale of Fair and Excellent, use the scale Worse, Same, and Better. What you're doing is comparing each of the comparables to your house.

You see now that even if you rated your house excellent in all categories, you still may come across a property that is better than yours. You don't need to worry that the comparable is "more excellent." You just need to objectively note that it is in fact a better property than yours. And here's the important part: the more excellent property will rent for a higher price than yours.

Putting It Together

At best the information you've gathered will narrow the range of rent you might charge for the property. For an obvious example, let's take a situation where you've looked at two comparables and they match your house on the major criteria. The only difference is the number of rooms.

House A	two bedrooms	$1,000 monthly rent
House B	four bedrooms	$1,500 monthly rent
Your house	three bedrooms	?

It's clear that your house is bigger than House A and smaller than House B. All other things being equal, your rent should be somewhere between $1,000 and $1,500.

A similar example can be created regarding the less objective factors. Say someone is asking $1,200 per month rent for a house that on your evaluation sheet you rated in better condition than your house. All other things being equal, it is unlikely that you could charge $1,200 per month rent. You would have to charge a lower figure. However, if you found a house for rent at $2,000 in a school district that most people thought is not as good as the district your house is in, then it is likely that you could charge more than $2,000 per month.

What's the Bedroom Worth?

At this point you may ask how much more you can charge for that third bedroom or the second bathroom. Or how much will you have to lower the rent because you're not in the excellent school district. Unfortunately the answer to that question in any particular area for any one of the criteria we're talking about requires more research and knowledge than can be provided here. Fortunately it doesn't really matter that much since you can do enough research to make a pretty educated estimate of what your rent should be. The key is to research the rental market enough to get a good feel for what people are charging.

If you're able to find ten properties that are vaguely similar to yours that are for rent, divide them into two lists of better and worse. In some cases a few of the criteria will be better while other criteria in the same house will be worse. Try to get a general impression of whether overall the comparable is better or worse than your house. You can also try to evaluate the comparables to narrow the focus on your house:

House	Bedrooms	Condition	Rent
House A	three bedrooms	worse than your house	$1,000
House B	three bedrooms	better than House A but still worse than your house	$1,100

Based on this example you can begin to see that you will probably want to offer your three-bedroom house at a rent higher than $1,100.

But what if House A had four bedrooms and was still being offered for $1,000 monthly rent? There are a few possibilities:

- Condition is more important in your market than bedroom count.
- The fourth bedroom doesn't have much value (discussed later).
- The owner of one of the comparables has incorrectly priced the house.

These types of studies, often called comparative market analysis, are imprecise at best and rely heavily on the information available and the experience of the person—usually a real estate agent—doing them. By looking at enough houses and apartments being offered for rent, you will be able to find an answer to the earlier question.

Let's discuss the value of extra rooms. With respect to multiple rooms of the same type—bedrooms, bathrooms, garages—beyond a certain minimum acceptable number, the more you have the less valuable the excess ones are. For most families, the master bedroom is a necessity. A sufficient number of bedrooms that allows for the separation of children by gender is the next most important thing. A bedroom for each child is nice but not absolutely necessary. Obviously these criteria will be driven by personal values and the amount of money available to spend. But in any given situation, that fourth bedroom will likely be less valuable than the third one. For example:

House A	Two bedrooms	$800 monthly rent
House B	Three bedrooms	$1,000
House C	Four bedroom	$1,100
House D	Five bedrooms	$1,100

Notice in this example the third bedroom adds more value than the fourth. It is entirely possible in your market area that a fifth bedroom may have no additional value at all. Bathrooms and garages should be considered in the same way.

The value of other rooms such as the kitchen and living room is related to whether or not there is one in the first place. For example, some houses do not have formal dining rooms. All other things being equal, such a house would be worth less than one with a formal dining room.

Size, functionality, and condition are the important criteria that determine how much a room will be worth in comparison to the same room in another house.

Finally, one way to analyze the data is to do a little simple math as illustrated in Chapter 19.

Vacancy and Collection Loss / Effective Gross Income

Landlords and professional property managers always assume that they will not collect 100 percent of the rent, 100 percent of the time. Tenants may move out without paying rent. The rental unit may be vacant for major repairs or while it's being advertised between tenants. In apartment buildings, a percentage of the gross income is used as a vacancy and collection loss figure. In single-family house rentals, you should use one month's rent as a projected loss.

Since the pro forma is done for one year, you are using eleven months' worth of rent for your Effective Gross Income or the income you have to work with. Even though you may not lose one month's rent each year, you might have a two-month vacancy between tenants at the end of a two-year rental.

Determine Your Expenses

You've now estimated what you think you'll charge for rent (i.e., the Potential Gross Income) and what you have to work with (i.e., the Effective Gross Income). Remember, at this point you haven't tested the market by advertising the house, so this is still only an estimate.

Consider the expenses the tenants will pay directly. For example, you will most likely pay the taxes and insurance on the property. You may make the tenants pay their own electricity and heating costs. There is no universally correct way to do this. Your research into comparable rentals will give you an idea of what is common practice in your area. The lease will spell out what you will provide and what the tenant is responsible for.

Fixed expenses

These are expenses you'd have whether you rented the property or not. The two expenses that are always placed in this category are property taxes and property insurance, including any additional costs of insurance to rent the property. As fixed expenses that will not vary with the tenants, you should assume that you will pay these two items.

Variable expenses

This covers pretty much everything else associated with the property. Some of these expenses will vary with whether or not the property is rented and with the use of the property by the tenant. They will sometimes vary by season and the part of the country you're in. Whether these expenses are even a consideration will depend on your particular house. Following is a list of the most common regular expenses associated with homeownership that must be considered when renting your house:

- Electricity
- Gas
- Oil
- Water
- Sewage
- Lawn and landscaping
- Common or homeowners' association charges
- Maintenance
- Telephone
- Cable TV
- Alarm System
- Garbage collection
- High-speed Internet connection

Think about these:

- Consider what suits you best.
- Consider the expectations of tenants in your particular market area.
- Be realistic about what you can take care of personally.
- A lease does not control a tenant's behavior.
- In the end it's what you and the tenant negotiate.
- If the tenant pays the expense directly, it will not be counted in the pro forma. If it's included in the rent, it will be.

Electricity

The most common bill paid directly by any tenant is electricity. Electrical usage will vary widely from tenant to tenant, especially if the house is equipped with electric heat and/or central air conditioning. The tenant should be responsible for paying this directly to the utility company.

Contact your utility company and advise them of your intention to rent the property. Find out the steps needed to transfer billing and payment directly to a tenant. It will probably be necessary for the tenant to contact the company to arrange for the transfer of service. Be aware that if the tenant moves out of the area when their rental is over, it will be very difficult for you or the utility company to collect on an unpaid utility bill. The utility company may attempt to collect from you. Check with your attorney as to your responsibility in such a case; however, it may be easier to pay the bill from the security deposit. The conditions for return of the security deposit should include sufficient time for the last utility bill to have been paid and payment verified by the utility company. Because of privacy regulations, you may have to obtain verification through the tenant.

Gas

Gas may be used to heat the house or only for cooking. Natural gas will be metered and propane gas in a tank will be paid by delivery. In either case, handle the transfer of gas service, billing, and payment in the same way as electrical service and billing. With propane gas, the tenant may want reimbursement for unused gas that they've paid for but haven't used when they move out.

Oil

Many homes use oil as the fuel for heat and making hot water. If your house uses oil, you'll want to arrange for billing and payment to be taken care of directly by the tenant. Heating, cooling, and the use of hot water are among the most variable property expenses as they are highly dependent on personal preference. As with electricity and gas, contact your oil supplier early in the process to find out what steps are necessary to transfer billing to the tenant. The company may want you to guarantee payment or may require the tenant to pay on delivery. Make sure you are protected financially and that the tenant is informed how delivery, billing, and payment will be handled. As with propane gas, the tenant reasonably may want to be reimbursed for oil that they've paid for but haven't used when they move out.

Water

Inform the tenant if water is supplied through a well; the cost will be part of the billing for electricity. If the water is metered, contact the water supplier to get the billing transferred to the tenant. As with the gas and electric, this may involve setting a date to read the meter for transfer of usage. If you live in a part of the country where regular watering is necessary to maintain an attractive lawn, you may want to retain payment of the water bill. You don't want the tenant deciding not to keep your lawn in good shape.

Sewage

If you handle sewage through a septic system on your property, you may want to get it cleaned out if it hasn't been in a while. If your sewage is handled by your city or county, you probably pay for sewage disposal through regular real estate tax, a sewage tax based on your assessed value, or a fee based on actual usage. Generally these charges should be included in the rent, especially if they are a part of the tax bill. If sewage use is calculated by some sort of metering, you can charge the tenant separately.

Lawn and landscaping

How do you handle this now? Can it continue to be taken care of in the same way? Remember that you want the house to be well maintained even if you're not going to continue to market it while you're renting it. One summer of landscape neglect can mean extra costs to restore the lawn and gardens.

Here are some of the more likely possibilities:

- You currently handle all the landscaping chores and are going to be living close enough to continue to do so.
- You currently use a professional landscaping and/or lawn service and want to continue that.
- The tenant fancies herself a gardener and offers to take care of this in exchange for a lower rent.

Landscaping is long-term maintenance and your responsibility whether or not the house is occupied. Having the tenant assume that responsibility is not a wise choice because your version of acceptable maintenance may be very different from his. If the tenant would like to do a little gardening and you have the space, set aside a vegetable or flower garden area for that purpose.

Common or homeowners' association charges

In certain types of subdivisions or planned communities, there may be homeowners' association fees due each month. In a condominium or cooperative, there will almost certainly be so-called common charges or association fees. It is unlikely that you would be able to transfer the payment of this directly to your tenant. You would probably have to indicate to the tenant that the common charges are so much a month and that they would have to pay you so you could pay the association. The one advantage of this is that the lease would be written so that any increase in common charges would be passed on to the tenant.

While this is possible to do, it is probably easier to just build the common charges into the rent and pay them yourself. Most of the homeowners' association fees go to maintaining the common areas, exterior of buildings including your unit, and taxes. These are all costs that you would bear yourself if you were renting a traditional single-family house with no homeowners' fees. Although not included in the pro forma, this would be placed in the fixed charges section along with taxes and insurance.

Tenants can pay extra fees such as golf course or pool charges if they wish to use those facilities. Since you are the owner, depending on condominium and cooperative procedures, you may have to collect the fees from the tenant and pay them to the association.

Maintenance

Maintaining any rental property is generally the responsibility of the owner/landlord. Preventive maintenance, like furnace cleaning and prompt repairs when necessary, maintain the value of the premises and fulfill the obligation of the owner to provide a safe and habitable environment for the tenant. If possible, the cost of maintenance and repairs should be covered by the rent. They must also be accounted for in the projected budget.

Review two or three years' worth of maintenance and repair bills for your house. Search your memory for those repairs and maintenance chores you may have made yourself and determine if you will still be able to do them or if you will hire people.

You can easily estimate preventive maintenance items like furnace and chimney cleaning. Corrective maintenance (i.e., repairs) is harder to estimate because you can't predict the future. Account for the amount you know and then give yourself a little cushion for unforeseen repairs. Tenants may be harder on a house than you are and as a house gets older it tends to need more attention.

Telephone

Telephone is always a tenant expense. It does not need to be included in the pro forma budget.

Cable TV

Cable TV, as well as high-speed Internet connection, is a direct tenant expense. Check with the cable company about stopping your service. Advise the new tenants whom to call to begin service.

Alarm system

If you have an alarm system built into the house, you pay for monitoring of break-ins, fire, and possibly furnace shutoffs. An alarm system is primarily for the safety of the residents but may also provide safety for the structure.

You may handle the cost by paying for it yourself, having the tenant pay voluntarily, or requiring the tenant to pay. If you feel that the alarm system is important to protect the residence from fire or furnace failure, then you should pay for it yourself or try to get the tenant to pay for it. One approach would be to place a clause in the lease requiring the tenant to pay separately for the alarm system and see what happens. Be prepared to negotiate if necessary, perhaps offering to pay half.

For purposes of the pro forma, consider the full cost of the monitoring service an expense. You can always change it after the lease has been signed.

Garbage collection

If you have municipal garbage pickup, you most likely pay for it through your property taxes. If your area does not have municipal garbage pickup, explain to the prospective tenant that they will have to pay for private sanitation collection. When the lease is signed, give them the phone number of the sanitation company and be sure to contact the company yourself and advise them to switch billing to the tenant.

Snow removal

Snow removal expense is climate dependent. Depending on the size of your driveway and sidewalks, you may shovel it or use a snowblower, retain a regular plowing service on call, or wait for the neighborhood kids to come by and shovel. Snow removal, especially from the driveway, is generally for the convenience of the tenant, and therefore can be a tenant-paid expense.

As I discussed in the section on lease terms, the exception may be if your municipality requires that public sidewalks be kept free of snow and ice. In this case you may have to assume responsibility and include it in the rent.

Management fees

By the time you've finished reading, you will have decided whether or not to use a professional real estate manager to manage the rental of your house. If you decide to use a property manager, you need to build in an expense for the management fee. Review the chapter on using a property manager, then discuss fees with several managers and include an amount as an expense in your budget.

Reserves

In most rental properties there are items that need to be replaced periodically (e.g., a roof, cooking stove in a rental apartment, or the water heater). These items will not have to be replaced each year but will not last as long as the life of the building itself. A prudent landlord / property manager will include a certain amount of money each year in the budget to cover the cost of these items.

You will probably not be renting your house out for a long enough period of time to worry about these items. In any case, whether you rented the house or not, you would be replacing these items in order to maintain the house in good condition for sale. You don't need to include any expenses in the traditional reserve for replacement items in your pro forma.

Assuming that you don't specifically budget for repairs in the variable expenses, it would be prudent to set aside some money each month for unexpected repairs such as the plumbing or heating service calls. You probably won't have to spend this money on a monthly basis so it can accumulate to cover repairs as necessary. The amount you set aside is arbitrary. The idea is to build up a little cushion of money designated for unexpected property expenses.

Net Operating Income / Cash Flow

At this point, you can total your expenses and subtract the total from the Effective Gross Income. The result is the Net Operating

Income. Next, subtract your total annual mortgage payment and what you have left is what is referred to as Cash Flow. Remember that you have already subtracted real estate taxes and insurance so the only thing you need to subtract here is the mortgage payment itself. There are three possible outcomes of this calculation:

- Positive cash flow—All your expenses are covered and you have money left.
- Zero cash flow—You take away no money but all your expenses are covered.
- Negative cash flow—Not all of your expenses are covered by the rent.

Obviously you're hoping that renting the house will cover all expenses. And if you're fortunate you might take away a little cash each month, too. But even if you are in a negative cash flow situation, remember that you would have to pay all the expenses on the house out of your pocket if it were not rented.

There are two notes of caution regarding a negative cash flow situation. First, you cannot automatically assume that you can charge a higher rent to cover expenses. As pointed out in the section on the wrong way to set the rent, the market, not your expenses, will determine what you can charge for rent.

Second, if your negative cash flow is high enough, it may pay you to sell the house now for less than you want. This way you avoid generating more losses waiting to sell the house at a higher price. (See real estate math in Chapter 19.)

The Budget Bottom Line

Creating a pro forma or estimated budget is a first step in deciding whether to rent the property and then manage the property. You will probably revise the budget several times as you go along and reality intrudes on your projections. In fact, as you work on the pro forma you might do what the professionals do: Create several different budget scenarios. Do a conservative estimate where the rent is low and the expenses are high. Then do a more optimistic budget where the rent is at the upper end of your estimates and the expenses are relatively low.

Once you understand the pro forma, you can condense the budget into a simple income/outgo format.

Keep Good Records

It's vital to keep good records of income and expenses for the property. Ideally you should start a separate checking account to deposit the rent and pay the bills. If you use computer software to track the income and expenses, make sure you properly back up your records. These will be important for income tax purposes as well as to see where you are financially.

CHAPTER EIGHT ACTION POINTS

☐ Prepare a pro forma to estimate income and expenses.

☐ Try different pro forma models with different expenses and income.

☐ Research local rents for your type of house.

☐ Review your expenses for one or two years.

☐ Research what is typically included and what is usually a tenant-paid item in your area.

☐ Revise the pro forma when you finally settle on a tenant and rent amount.

☐ Prepare a good recordkeeping system.

CHAPTER NINE

MAINTENANCE

Types of Maintenance

A PROPERTY USUALLY generates four kinds of maintenance. *Preventive maintenance* is maintenance that is done periodically to avoid more serious damage to the structure or equipment. Examples of preventive maintenance are exterior painting of wood siding to prevent rot, or cleaning the chimney to prevent a fire.

Routine maintenance is done periodically as a matter of upkeep. Mowing the lawn and trimming the hedges are routine maintenance items.

Corrective maintenance is the maintenance needed to repair something and bring it back to its working condition. Fixing a leaky faucet or a broken air-conditioning compressor is corrective maintenance. Structurally, replacing termite-damaged wood is corrective maintenance.

Deferred maintenance is maintenance that should be done but is not. That exterior paint job you should have done as preventive maintenance becomes an item of deferred maintenance when it is obvious that you didn't do it. Deferred maintenance that can be seen can reduce both the sale and rental value of a house. From a landlord's perspective, deferred maintenance that is unseen can result in costly repairs or become a safety issue (e.g., if the furnace has not been cleaned). From a seller's perspective, deferred maintenance that is not obvious may get picked up if the buyer has a home inspection done, potentially reducing the value of the property.

It can also surface as a safety issue that must be disclosed to a potential buyer.

Safety First

The most important maintenance issues relate to safety. This has been discussed in Chapter 7, but the importance of this subject cannot be overemphasized. You have a legal responsibility to maintain the rental property in a safe, habitable condition. You must know and obey all rules and regulations regarding safety codes and regulations. Remember that the difference between an injury or death that occurs because of an accident and one that occurs because a safety regulation was not followed is the difference between civil and possibly criminal liability.

There may be many safety issues in your area that apply to rental properties. Some may only apply to commercial or large multifamily buildings. Whatever the case, you need to know and comply with the ones that apply to your situation. Typical safety concerns may involve:

- Fire prevention and warning equipment, such as extinguishers and detectors
- Exits
- Lighting
- Illegal rooms, such as basement bedrooms
- Improperly built structures, such as decks
- Electrical hazards
- Heating equipment
- Fireplaces
- Environmental hazards

Some of these items have been covered, so this discussion will focus on more direct safety items.

Visit your local building department and ask for a copy of the fire and safety rules that apply to renting single-family homes. An official may be able to give you a summary of these regulations. Have the same discussion with a fire inspector at the local fire department. Depending on your municipality, there may be a jurisdictional split between what the fire officials and the building officials cover. A building inspector may remind you to install a smoke detector. A fire inspector may point out the need to unblock exits. You may be able to arrange for the building inspector or fire inspector to inspect the property and make recommendations for tenant safety.

People rent houses, apartments, and commercial buildings throughout the country with few if any problems regarding safety issues. The key is in finding out what the law says and obeying it.

Once you become aware of any safety violation by the tenant or other safety issue that develops while the house is rented, your liability window has opened, and you must respond immediately and appropriately.

 tip **DO THE SAFE THING**

Suppose you find out through routine furnace maintenance that there is a carbon monoxide leak and it will take a few days to get the repair completed or a new furnace installed. Move the tenants into a motel at your expense and if necessary rebate the rent for those days they are unable to occupy the house. Even if the leak is small and can be taken care of temporarily by opening a window, get the tenants out of the house. This is perhaps a drastic scenario but you must understand the seriousness of safety issues with respect to tenants. This example is based on two cases; one in which a child died and another in which rent was withheld for several months.

Deliver What You Promised

Important points to consider:

- The lease is a promise.
- Be careful what you promise.
- Do what you said you would do even if it's not in the lease.
- Think twice before committing anything to writing.

The promise you make in the lease is to provide a safe and habitable environment for the tenant. Beyond that you may be inclined to make certain statements or promises. Be careful what you say and how you say it. A casual remark by you may be interpreted by the tenant as a promise.

During the course of lease negotiations you say, "I was thinking of painting the place." The tenant hears "Oh! Good! The landlord is going to paint the place before we move in."

Obviously there may be things that you have to and want to commit to as part of the lease negotiations. If repainting the house is a good idea for the eventual sale as well as the rental, then go ahead and tell the prospective tenants that's what you're going to do. Then do it before they move in.

As with any negotiation, be clear on what you say and what is understood by the other party. Do not make promises as an inducement unless you intend to keep them, and follow through promptly on anything that you have told the tenant you would do.

Do It Yourself

One of the ways small rental property owners keep expenses low is by doing most of the maintenance and repairs themselves. In your situation, whether you can or choose to do this will depend on location, time, skill, and cost versus savings. If you will be living nearby while the house is being rented, you may be able to respond to maintenance complaints as well as take care of routine maintenance chores. Even if you are living nearby, the question of available time will determine how much if any of the maintenance you will be able to handle. And finally do you have the skill to maintain the property, and to what extent? You might be a wonderful painter but not so good with plumbing. Only you can answer the question as to your skill level.

Safety considerations also play a part in deciding whether to do it yourself. It is doubtful that anyone can be seriously hurt by a bad paint job as long as you remember to leave the windows open. On the other hand, a house can burn down from an amateur electrical installation.

What Is Your Time Worth?

One of the things people who self-manage their investment properties often do not consider is the value of their own time. Assuming that you are living close by the property so that you can actually do some or all of the maintenance, should you? Things to consider:

- Do you have the skills?
- Do you have the tools?
- Could you be earning enough money to be doing something else and hiring people?
- Are people available to do the jobs you need done?
- Are the finances of the property so tight that you must do the maintenance yourself?

This is not a definitive list but addressing some of these questions may help you decide if and when to do it yourself.

A TALE OF TWO DIARIES
Excerpt of the diary of the owner who has decided to self-maintain the property:
MONDAY, 6:00 A.M.: Stopped by the house to shovel the snow off the sidewalk.
SATURDAY, 10:00 A.M.: Went to the house to fix the leaking faucet.
SUNDAY, 3:00 P.M.: Tenants called that one of the sinks is stopped up. Went over to unclog it.
MONDAY, 3:00 A.M.: Tenant called to say the furnace went out; went over to check it out. Had to call furnace repair company and wait until the man got there so I could authorize the repairs.

Excerpt of the diary of the owner who has hired out all the repair and maintenance tasks:
MONDAY, 8:00 A.M.: Drove by the house to check if the sidewalk had been shoveled. It had.
SATURDAY, 10:00 A.M.: Called tenant to tell them the plumber would be there on Monday to fix the leaky faucet.

continued

SUNDAY, 3:00 P.M.: Tenants called that one of the sinks is stopped up and overflowed. I told tenant to mop up the water and that I would call the plumber first thing in the morning.

MONDAY, 3:00 A.M.: Tenant called to say the furnace went out. I told the tenant to call the furnace repair company directly and to call me when a repair person arrived. I got a call an hour later and authorized the necessary repair work.

Excerpt of the diary of an owner who hired a professional manager to manage the property:

FRIDAY: Got my monthly report advising me of any repair and maintenance issues on the property.

Hiring Contractors

The alternative to doing it yourself is to hire people. Remember that the type of contractors you're going to hire and the arrangements you make with them will vary with the particular type of maintenance you need done.

For routine maintenance, make arrangements with lawn and snow removal contractors to provide service on an ongoing basis. Get a cost estimate from two or three contractors for their services. Ask your neighbors for recommendations.

Contractors for these types of services often like to be paid each time they come to the house. They are used to dealing with the homeowner and not a tenant. Make arrangements with them to bill you or to pay them monthly or on some other schedule. Check with your tenant to see if the service was actually performed before you pay.

Preventive Maintenance

While you're setting up your rental "business," remember to make a schedule for the preventive maintenance tasks that you will have to arrange. Every house is different but things like a furnace cleaning, chimney cleaning, water softener service, and septic tank pumping may need to be scheduled. It's usually simply a matter of making a call to arrange the service. But as a landlord, you have another step:

Let the tenant know when the service is going to happen. In today's world where an entire family will likely be out of the house during the day, you will probably need to call the tenant first to see when someone might be home if access to the house is needed. The alternative is to let the tenant know ahead of time that you will be coming into the house to let a service person in on a certain day.

Remember that the lease requires you to give the tenant his or her privacy. It allows you access to the house only in emergencies and with prior permission of the tenant. Try to take care of most of these preventive maintenance chores before you rent the house.

Corrective Maintenance

Routine repairs like leaky faucets required little more than a call to the plumber when you were living in your house. Being a landlord and taking care of routine repairs requires a bit more planning. Think about whether you or the tenant will call the repair person when needed. Decide who will be present while repairs are made and how the repair person will be paid. Have the tenant call you. You can make arrangements to meet the plumber at the property. Let the tenant know when you'll be going into the house, and that you'll pay when the service is complete.

An alternative if somewhat less controlled way of handling these types of repairs is to let the tenant take responsibility. Give the tenant the name and phone numbers of various contractors that you use. If a problem develops, the tenant calls the contractor and makes all the necessary arrangements to have the repair completed. The tenant also calls you to let you know what happened. You contact the company and arrange to pay the bill directly.

A major consideration of how you handle these types of corrective maintenance repairs will be your physical availability to be at the property. You may have little choice, but you should consider carefully giving over authority to the tenant to decide when to call a repair person.

A compromise solution may be to have the tenant call you first with a repair issue, allowing you to make the decision of what to do.

If you feel the situation warrants it, you can instruct the tenant to call the repair person and schedule the repair.

Emergencies

Have a plan to deal with emergencies. The type of emergencies that you need to be concerned about generally relate to structural or mechanical issues. For example, the furnace breaks down at three o'clock in the morning on the coldest night of the year. By contrast, a leaky drain that can be dealt with using a bucket until morning is not an emergency. Take some steps to minimize confusion and lost time in the event of an emergency. Discuss with the tenant a plan for handling emergencies. Give the tenant several phone numbers where you can be reached day or night, along with a list of contractors' phone numbers.

In the event of an emergency, respond as quickly as you can. Tenants expect to always have a safe and habitable environment and that any repair will be made immediately, even if you are dependent on a repairperson's schedule. You need to always show your concern for the tenant and the property and make every attempt to get the repair done as quickly as possible. You also need to keep the tenant informed of the status of the repair work.

CHAPTER NINE ACTION POINTS

- ☐ You are responsible for all forms of maintenance on the property.
- ☐ Maintenance items related to safety are your most important priority.
- ☐ Good maintenance is owed to the tenant and will maintain the value of the property for eventual sale.
- ☐ You need to decide what if any maintenance you can do yourself as opposed to hiring someone.
- ☐ Prepare for emergencies.

CHAPTER TEN
PROTECT THE PROPERTY

AS THE LANDLORD there are a few things you can do at the beginning, during, and at the end of the relationship with your tenant to keep property damage to a minimum. Assume that the tenant will be responsible and fair and will take care of your property since it will be his dwelling for a time. But be aware that even a responsible tenant will rarely care for your property as well as you do.

People also have different standards of care and what constitutes clean. You have a limited ability to dictate how a tenant lives in the house as long as she is not damaging it. But you may find that at the end of the lease the oven that was in spotless condition when you rented the house is now in need of sandblasting. You should also keep in mind that you may be continuing to market the property while you are renting it, so ongoing protection of the property can become as important as minimizing the amount of repairs you may have to do when the tenant moves out.

Inspect the Property with the Tenant

You and your new tenant have agreed to all the terms of the lease and the lease has been signed and you've received the security deposits and first month's rent (and last month's if you required it). It is now time to schedule an inspection of the property with the tenant.

This is a simple walk-through of all the rooms in the house including the basement and any outbuildings. Make clear to the tenant that this is as much, if not more, for their protection than yours. Explain to them that the goal of the inspection is to see if anything needs repairing before the tenant moves in. You want to establish the condition of the property at the beginning of the lease because you would not want to hold the tenant responsible for any damage that pre-existed their tenancy. Here are a few hints in setting up the inspection:

- Arrange a mutually agreeable time to meet at the property.
- Try to have all adult tenants present at the inspection.
- The house should be in its rentable condition. If you're renting it unfurnished, your furniture should be gone.
- Take care of all needed repairs, cleanup, and painting before the inspection, if possible.
- Conduct the inspection in daylight, if possible.
- Bring a notebook and pen to take notes.

Remember as you discuss the inspection with the tenant you are doing nothing more than establishing a baseline of the condition of the property so that there are no arguments at the end of the lease regarding damages to the house or land.

Photographs and Video

You may want bring a still or video camera with you. So as not to take time during the inspection itself, arrive a little early at the property and take a series of photos or videos while you're waiting for the tenant. You'll have the camera with you and can tell them what you did. If the tenant points out something that is not in proper repair or is damaged, take a picture. If the tenant wants a copy of the video or photographs, provide them.

Use a Checklist

A checklist will help you to remember everything you want to look at. It will also provide a record of the condition the house was in when you rented it. If you use a formal checklist, you can have the tenants initial it and give them a copy. This is another way to ensure

fewer arguments at the end of the lease as to the original condition of the property.

Since every house is different, it's difficult to provide you with a "one size fits all" checklist. Here are a few hints at how you can approach creating your own.

List each room of the house.

List each fixture in each bathroom.

List each major appliance separately.

List the basement, garage, and any other accessory buildings.

Leave room for notes after each entry.

Conduct the Inspection

Meet the tenants at the property. You have your checklist and you're ready to go. There's no right or wrong way to do this. Start at the front door and go room by room with the tenant. Note any existing damage to walls, floors, doors, trim molding, and windows. If any window treatments or window hardware is staying, make a note of that. Note any damage the tenant points out.

In the bathrooms run each faucet, shower, and bathtub fixture. Work the stoppers and make sure each fixture drains well. Make sure the toilets are working properly. This allows you to check on the condition of each fixture and to demonstrate to the tenant that they are all working properly. Make a note of any cracks or significant scratches in sinks, showers, and tubs. In the kitchen check every appliance and fixture in front of the tenant. Make note of any damage or scratches to countertops, sinks, and appliances.

You should have previously taken photos of each plumbing fixture, countertop, and appliance showing its condition. You want to be sure there is a record that there was no damage at the time you rented the house.

Don't forget the outside of the house, the land, and any buildings the tenants might be using as part of their lease. Include notes and photos of the outside as part of your inspection checklist. And check out any equipment like lawn mowers that you might be leaving for the tenant's use.

If there is no damage in a room, write down words to that effect. At the end of the inspection tour, have the tenant sign or initial the inspection checklist under the word *agreed* or *accepted*, date it, and offer to send him or her a copy. Send the copy promptly and put the original in your lease file together with any photos or videos you took.

Personal Visits

While the property is rented, without being intrusive or violating the terms of the lease, take every opportunity to visit the property. A rental property or the neighborhood it's in can change rapidly; and often not for the better. Here are a few ways to legitimately visit the property on a regular basis:

- Collect the rent in person each month.
- Be there for any scheduled maintenance or repair work.
- Inspect the property after any lawn maintenance is done.
- Plan to be present for all buyer visits to the property.
- Drive by regularly and never at the same time.

This last one may sound as if you're spying. In a way you are, but it's your property and all you're doing is keeping an eye on it. For example, suppose your tenants are running an unauthorized car repair business in your garage on Saturdays and Sundays. If all you do is collect the rent and drive by occasionally on the way home from work, you'll never know what they're doing.

You want to maintain a balance between allowing the tenants the privacy they're paying for and your right to monitor your property. Avoid unannounced visits unless you have a legitimate reason to stop by without calling first.

While you're at it, pay attention to what's going on in the neighborhood when you visit your property. A change for better or worse in the neighborhood may signal a decision point regarding sale of the house.

tip

THE PRICE OF ABSENCE

A landlord rented his house to a tenant who had a side business of repairing cars on the weekend. The tenant assured the landlord that he would only repair cars on Saturdays and he would do all the work inside the garage. He promised that no cars would be stored on the property except for his family's personal vehicles. The landlord seldom drove by the property.

About six months after renting the property, the landlord received a notice of violation of the zoning ordinance for running a business in a residential area. He was notified to appear in court to answer the citation.

The tenant had been working on cars in the driveway using noisy machinery. Apparently this went on at least two or three nights a week and all day Saturdays and Sundays. One or more of the neighbors had complained to the town.

A hefty fine was levied in court. The landlord ordered the tenant to stop working on the cars. The tenant missed a few months rent payments whereupon the landlord had to begin eviction proceedings.

Enforce the Rules

When you wrote the lease, you tried to include all pertinent rules for use of the house and land. You hope that the tenant will follow these rules. What do you do if they don't? You enforce the rules. Being a landlord is work, but it can be interesting and lucrative. And it doesn't have to be stressful; that is, until you must deal with a tenant who breaks the rules or damages the property. If the rules regarding use of the property made sense in the first place, they should be enforced without hesitation or second-guessing. In many cases, the use restrictions you've placed on the property are either to comply with local laws and/or to protect the property from damage. For example, the prohibition against repairing cars in the garage and the driveway, regardless of whether it's being done for personal or commercial purposes. is to avoid your garage and driveway looking and smelling like an auto repair shop.

What steps should you take to enforce a provision in the lease that the tenant is violating? First, have a talk with the tenant, preferably with a witness present. Do not make any threats. Simply state the provisions in the lease, suggest that they may have not read the lease carefully or simply forgotten and that you would appreciate them stopping the prohibited activity immediately.

If the activity does not stop, the next step is to send them a registered letter with a return receipt requested. Keep a copy of the letter and the receipt when you get it back. The letter again should tell them to stop the activity immediately. Specifically note in the letter that the activity is prohibited by the terms of the lease. Make no threats. If they continue with the prohibited activity, see your attorney to initiate eviction proceedings. And welcome to the dark side of landlording.

CHAPTER TEN ACTION POINTS

☐ Make a record of the condition of the property when the tenant moves in.

☐ Inspect the property with the tenant.

☐ Visit the property and the neighborhood occasionally.

☐ Be sure to enforce the rules for use of the property, particularly those that if violated might cause damage to the house or land.

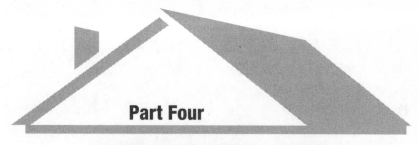

Part Four

INSURANCE AND TAX ISSUES

INSURANCE AND LIABILITY

YOU SHOULD REALIZE that you can be sued by anyone at anytime for anything. Ask yourself these important questions:

- How can I minimize the likelihood of being sued?
- How can I maximize my chances of winning a lawsuit if I am sued?
- How can I protect myself from financial disaster if I lose a lawsuit?

Liability—Who Is Responsible?

To make sense of insurance issues, you need to understand a little about liability. Liability is basically the legal term for responsibility. If you hit another car with your car, you may be liable. However, you may be found not liable if you were within the speed limit and obeying all traffic laws and the other car ran a stop sign.

Another example is a man tripping over a doorway step and injuring himself. Was the doorway properly marked and lit? Was it an unusual doorway step, maybe unusually high? Was the man drunk? These are a few of the questions asked in court to determine liability. In some cases the victim has to bear a portion of the liability. So the drunken man tripping over the unusually high step might have to bear a portion of the liability because of his condition.

Liability issues can be complicated. Accidents happen. Situations exist that can cause people harm. Judges and juries are unpredictable in how they assign liability. Your goal should be to eliminate to the maximum possible extent any situation or condition that could cause injury to your tenant or their visitors.

Your responsibility is primarily physical (i.e., eliminating or reducing physical hazards on the property). You cannot control the behavior of your tenant, although the law recognizes the concept of attractive nuisance. So the tenant who fell off the cliff on your property walked to the edge of the cliff herself. But you hadn't put a fence up. You both may share the liability for the accident.

Criminal Liability

If someone is injured as a result of your breaking the law, you may be guilty of criminal liability. You may be charged with a crime depending on the severity of the injury and the law you broke. It does not relieve you of civil liability, which is usually handled through monetary compensation.

Your first goal in preparing your house and land for rent is to make sure the property is in compliance with all building, safety, fire, and electrical codes. Codes vary from state to state and town to town, but there are some common things that most codes cover. Refer to the discussion of these items in Chapter 7. Remember even though you're renting a single-family house and not a multistory apartment building, rental situations may be subject to different codes than owner-occupied homes. You may be able to get the building inspector to visit your house and determine if you are in compliance. If not, you may need to hire someone who specializes in safety inspections. This may not be your ordinary home inspector. Inquire carefully and be clear on the kind of inspection you want.

Injuries or deaths that can be traced to illegal or noncompliant conditions can result in criminal liability and insurance companies may refuse to cover the civil monetary awards, so compliance is your first priority in reducing your liability.

Civil Liability

Civil liability cases are usually based on an injury or death that can be traced to someone else's action or inaction, where no law was broken. The compensation is typically monetary. If you as a landlord didn't break a law and do anything wrong, how could a tenant sue you and win? Say there's a loose piece of carpeting in the living room and two days after the tenant moves in, she trips and hurts herself badly. Most likely there's no law that says the living room carpet has to be nailed down. On the other hand, it was an obvious safety hazard. If you want to further complicate the matter, let's say the tenant was in the house for six months when she fell and she had never complained about the loose carpet. The court might say she was partly responsible because after six months she should have said something to you and she should have been well aware of the hazard. On the other hand, you might need to prove that the hazard existed since she moved in. Furthermore the question arises, if you knew about it, why didn't you fix it? And that's why lawyers earn their money.

The point of this rather convoluted story is to illustrate one fact: as a landlord you need to take every step to minimize your liability due to any hazardous conditions that you are aware of in your house or on your property. The solution to the previous case is that it should never have happened. The carpet should have been nailed or glued down before the tenants moved in.

As you prepare your house for rent, take a careful walk around the house and the property. Bring a friend or family member with you. Make note of the following:

- Tripping hazards in the house
- Exposed sharp metal, glass, or other edges
- Damage to any appliance, doorway, counter, cabinet that could cause injury.
- Damaged railings or falling hazards requiring railings
- Holes, loose pavers, uneven steps, and other outside tripping hazards
- Junk, debris, equipment, tools that are going to remain on the property and may cause an attractive nuisance, especially for children

This is by no means a complete list. Be alert to any hazard in the house or around the property. Fix, eliminate, clean up, or lock away all the hazards you can. If a hazard is too expensive to repair and the risk of injury is low, you may have to live with it. And no matter what you do, accidents can happen. Your goal, to the maximum possible extent, is to prevent accidents.

Make the Tenant Responsible

The lease may contain provisions that make the tenant responsible for certain things such as snow and ice removal from the sidewalk. Say the postal delivery person slips and falls on the icy sidewalk that the tenant didn't get a chance to clean. You're off the hook, right? Maybe. If a lawsuit is initiated, it is likely that you as the property owner will be sued. You will have to prove that it was the tenant's responsibility for keeping the walkway clean. And even if the case goes to trial, a judge or jury could find that you as the owner bear ultimate responsibility for enforcing the terms of the lease. Try to make the tenant responsible for snow and ice removal if that makes sense but be aware that such a provision may not relieve you of responsibility.

THE RULES FOR LIABILITY ARE SIMPLE:
CONTROL IT: e.g., emergency lightning.
ELIMINATE IT: e.g., cover the swimming pool.
TRANSFER IT: e.g., insure against it.
LIVE WITH IT: e.g., the risk of something happening is so small that you can accept it.

Insurance

Property management professionals and investors evaluate the various risks associated with owning property. As mentioned in the sections about liability, an owner will try to eliminate risks where possible. The fact remains that even if you eliminated all controllable risks, there is still the possibility of an accident occurring and your being sued. That is generally why you have insurance.

For a simple one-family house rental, you generally want insurance coverage for two possibilities: damage to the property and injury to someone else. Assuming you rent the house unfurnished, you don't need to worry about personal property insurance. The tenants' personal property such as furniture will be their responsibility to insure through a renter's policy.

As an owner-occupant, you probably have a single comprehensive insurance policy that covers damage to the property from such things as fire and injury to someone while on your property, like the mailperson slipping on your icy walkway. You'll need to review your insurance coverage relative to renting the property. Notify your insurance company or agent that you intend to rent your house. The questions you want answered are:

- Does your current policy cover the house and liability if you rent it?
- Do you need different insurance, an additional policy, or some type of policy amendment to cover a rental situation?
- If your current policy covers rentals, should you increase your limits?
- If the cost of a new or amended policy is too high, can you reduce the costs by increasing your deductible?
- If you are renting the house furnished, how will your personal property be insured?

Do not skip this step of contacting your insurance company. If your policy excludes rental situations, you may not be covered in the event of an injury to someone or damage to the property. Have this conversation as early as possible when you're getting ready to rent the property. You will want to build into your operating budget the cost of any additional insurance that is necessary.

One final thought on obtaining insurance. If for some reason your insurance company will not insure a rental, find another insurance company and obtain a policy to cover your situation.

Minimize Your Personal Exposure

If you have substantial personal financial assets other than the house you're renting or even if you just want to further minimize your risk, you can consult with an attorney and discuss the possibility of incorporation. Corporation law can be very complicated. The simplified version for our purposes is that the law says that a corporation can be treated like a separate person. That person, the corporation, can own and rent a house. If something were to happen that involved a major liability claim as a result of renting the house, only the assets of the corporation would be at risk. It would be difficult if not impossible to go after your own personal assets that were not owned by the corporation.

It's expensive to form a corporation, however. Also certain types of corporations pay double taxes. If your only major asset is the house you're renting, it may not be worthwhile to go through the extra steps of forming and managing a corporation. On the other hand, if you have other property, investments, cash, or a high-paying job, you may wish to look into incorporation. Only an attorney can advise you on the pros and cons of incorporating in your particular situation and what type of corporation may suit your purposes. Note that you'll also want to consult an accountant to determine the tax implications of incorporation before you make a decision.

CHAPTER ELEVEN ACTION POINTS

☐ Be sure and obey all laws to reduce your criminal liability.

☐ Take all steps you can to reduce your civil liability.

☐ Review your insurance policy with your insurance agent / company.

☐ Secure additional insurance as needed.

☐ Review the possibility of incorporation with your attorney and accountant.

TAX ISSUES

Tax Laws That Work for You

THE FEDERAL GOVERNMENT uses its tax policy to encourage or discourage certain social and economic behavior. An example of this is the mortgage interest deduction on your income tax. The government thinks it's a good thing for people to own houses, so it helps by allowing that deduction. You purchased your house as your primary residence, but as soon as you start renting it out it becomes an investment. For tax purposes, the government treats your primary residence and an investment property differently.

The government thinks it's also good and necessary for the economy that people invest their money in various ways, including real estate. The house you are now renting is affected by the tax laws governing real estate investments. For the most part, these laws are designed to benefit the investor. As with most tax laws, they do make income tax filing and record-keeping a little more complicated. Consult with your accountant to discuss your particular situation.

Get an Accountant

Before you get too far down the road in the process of renting your house, interview at least three accountants who are familiar with small residential investment properties like one- to four-family houses. Choose an accountant and discuss what it is you intend to do. This chapter will give you an idea of some of the things you'll want to talk about. You also want some advice on keeping appropriate records for your rental property.

Once you've advised the accountant that you want her to do your tax work, she may be willing to meet with you at no cost for the initial consultation. Ask what her policy is or simply offer to pay for her time. After this initial consultation, the next time you see the accountant will be to file your income tax. Filing your taxes will be much easier if you ask a lot of questions and pay careful attention to what she tells you when you meet.

 A QUIZ
Do you know what depreciation is?
Do you know the cost recovery period on residential rental property?
Do you know how to calculate the capital gains on a property that you've depreciated and sold at a profit?
Do you know what, if any, personal expenses are deductible when managing a property?
If your answer to any question is no, you need an accountant. If your answer to all of these questions is no, you need an accountant *now*.

Income Taxes

The bad news is that rental income is subject to income taxes. In the vast majority of states, that will mean state and federal income taxes. In a few places, especially the larger cities, it may also mean city income taxes. The good news is that because rental income is derived from a business, the government allows certain costs associated with the property to be deducted from the income before calculating taxes. I discuss this in the next section. Because of the tax issues—both positive and negative—it is essential to keep records on rental income and expenses separate from your regular income and household records.

Deductions

As you already know, the government allows you to deduct your mortgage interest and the local property taxes that you pay on your house from your income when filing your taxes. This will not change when you begin renting your house except for the likelihood of having to file different tax forms to account for the rental property. What will be new is the likelihood that you will be able to deduct other expenses from your rental income. Maintenance costs for a rental property are generally deductible. It's unlikely that you will continue to pay the utility bills for the property, but if you did, they would be deductible.

You should keep good records, including bills and receipts for all expenses related to the rental property. Get specific instructions from your accountant on what records to keep. Do not allow your accountant to dismiss your question with the answer "just keep everything and we'll sort it out later." Based on that answer, you might not know to keep records of your travel expenses related to managing the property or the cost of newspaper ads advertising for a tenant.

You have been thinking like a homeowner. Admit your lack of knowledge to the accountant and ask for help in running this rental as a business. You may hope that you'll be able to sell the property quickly and therefore some of these things may not amount to much. If it takes longer than you expected, you'll be happy to have kept good records of all related expenses so that with your accountant's help you can take full advantage of the income tax code.

Depreciation

The government says that anyone whose business needs or uses equipment or buildings that wear out over time should have the opportunity to replace them by recovering the cost of the building or piece of equipment. Think about the simple example of a car rental business when all the cars wear out. There is no more business without the cars. So the government says that they will help you through the tax code to save money to replace the cars.

The same is true for a building. Buildings do wear out. And if you're in the business of renting out commercial or residential space, the government recognizes the need to recover the cost of that space as it wears out. Another term for depreciation is cost recovery.

The tax code says that you can deduct a certain portion of the original cost of your rental house each year from the income you make on the house before you calculate the taxes on that income. Depreciation is sometimes referred to as a paper loss because unlike other deductions you don't have to actually spend any money to qualify for the deduction, other than the original purchase price of the house. Not surprisingly, there are a number of rules. The two that concern us here are:

1. You can only depreciate the cost of the house, not the land.
2. The cost recovery period for residential rental property is 27.5 years.

Here's a simple example.

Original purchase price of your property = $343,000
House/land breakdown = $275,000/$68,000
Depreciation schedule: $275,000/27.5 years = $10,000 per year

As an example of the benefit, say you rented the house for $1,000 per month or a total of $12,000 for the year.

$12,000 income − $10,000 depreciation = $2,000 taxable income.

Because of depreciation, in this example, you would pay taxes on $2,000 instead of $12,000.

In case you wondering where the house/land split can be calculated, check with your tax assessor. Tax assessments usually are listed as house value / land value / total value. Unless you want to get an appraisal done, you can use the same proportion of house value to total value as the tax assessor uses.

There's a possibility of a further benefit. Suppose your income from the house is the $12,000 per year but your annual depreciation is $20,000. In effect, you have $8,000 in depreciation that you can't use. ($20,000 – $12,000 = $8,000). Under certain circumstances, you may be able to deduct some or all of the leftover $8,000 from other income that you have.

Overall depreciation is best left to the accountants to calculate and apply when you file your taxes. Discuss the effects of depreciation with your accountant. If you think that the depreciation will exceed the rental income from the house, ask the accountant about the possibility of deducting it against your other income.

Capital Gains—Primary Residence

A capital gain is profit on an investment. The government wants its share of capital gains profit through taxes. In order to encourage long-term investment (one year or more), the government has given favorable treatment to long-term capital gains by taxing them at a lower rate than ordinary income.

The government will tax the capital gain on your primary residence (i.e., the profit you make when selling). If you meet certain conditions, however, you will be able to deduct a portion of the capital gain and pay no tax on that portion. As with all deductions, check with your accountant about how this will apply to your situation. The general rules are as follows for the capital gain deduction on your primary residence:

- You lived in the home two of the last five years as your primary residence.
- A single owner can deduct up to $250,000 capital gain.
- Married owners can deduct up to $500,000 capital gain.
- There is no age limit.
- The deduction can be used multiple times as long as the primary residence and time frame rules are followed.

Understand that the capital gain means profit. So with some exceptions this means the difference between what you paid for the house and what you sold it for. Note the two-year time frame. If you end up renting your house for more than three years, you will have lost the two-year time period in which you had to have lived there as your primary residence. This may not matter if you have no profit on the ultimate sale of your house, but it could be costly if you bought your house many years ago and have realized a substantial gain in value.

Discuss this eventuality with your accountant when you begin to rent your property. It may be that the market will not come back to your expectations within a three-year time frame. Even so it may pay you to sell at a lower-than-expected price rather than pay capital gains tax.

Capital Gains—Investment Property

Long-term capital gains on investment property are still treated more favorably than regular income for tax purposes. Investment capital gains, however, are not treated the same as the gain on your primary residence. Capital gains on investment properties are taxed from the first dollar of profit. There is no overall deduction as there is with a gain on a primary residence.

A simplified calculation for capital gain on an investment property looks like this:

Sale price – Adjusted basis = Capital gain

Adjusted basis = Purchase price + Closing costs (on the purchase) + Capital improvements – Accrued (total) Depreciation

So the overall calculation becomes:

Capital gain = Sale price – Purchase price + Capital improvements + Closing costs (on the original purchase) – Accrued (total) depreciation

Say you bought a property for $200,000 and paid $10,000 in closing costs at the time of purchase. While you owned the property, you spent $15,000 in capital improvements. You also were able to deduct $5,000 per year in depreciation for the four years you owned the property. You now sell it for $250,000.

$200,000 (Purchase price)
+ $10,000 (Closing costs)
+ $15,000 (Capital improvements)
– $20,000 (Total depreciation, 4 years @ $5,000 per year)
= **$205,000 (Adjusted basis)**

$250,000 (Sale price)
– $205,000 (Adjusted basis)
= **$45,000 (Capital gain)**

There is one final calculation. Remember that the government has allowed you each year to deduct a certain amount of money that you didn't actually spend in the form of depreciation. Well, the government wants some of that back. In order to make this calculation, the government wants you to divide the total capital gain you made on the sale of your property into two parts: the actual gain and the gain you made through cost recovery (depreciation). In the example, you realized a total capital gain of $45,000. Of that, $20,000 was due to depreciation since you took a total of $20,000 during your ownership of the investment. The remainder, $25,000, was an actual gain due to the difference between your purchase price (as adjusted by closing costs and capital improvements) and the selling price. The government will tax the actual gain of $25,000 at one rate and the $20,000 due to depreciation at a different rate.

Depreciation is still a good deal because depreciation deductions are taken against income. You probably are paying at a higher tax bracket each year on your income than you will on the capital gains resulting from the total depreciation. Also remember that you had use of that money for all those years.

Depreciation—Standing in Two Worlds

The big issue with depreciation is how your gain will be treated when you sell the property. Depreciation taken while you're renting the house will have to be recovered as a capital gain when you sell it. But as long as you lived in the house for two years out of the last five, you'll be entitled to a large deduction on your capital gain.

Since every situation is different and tax laws do change from time to time, a book like this cannot give you specific tax advice nor detail in any way what the financial impact will be in your case.

Tax Deferred Exchanges

This is a fairly complicated subject and is primarily geared toward real estate investors. There is a part of the federal tax code referred to generically as 1031 Exchanges that permits a deferral of capital gains when selling investment properties. This is important if one of two things happens in your situation.

You may find that you've gone beyond the two years out of five time frame to qualify for the large primary residence capital gains tax deduction. Or on a more optimistic note you find that you like being a landlord and your finances allow you to continue to own rental property. In either case you may want a way to dispose of the property without paying capital gains taxes on it. The 1031 Exchange may allow you to do that.

The rules for exchanges are complicated. Most people have the idea that an exchange is something like trading baseball cards. The fact is that you do not need to find an exact property and owner who wishes to trade their property for yours. Exchanges are done through exchange agents who work with many owners of investment properties and identify properties for exchange. Exchanges are not available for primary residences but are geared toward investment properties. The program does generally require eventual payment of capital gains but you may be in a better financial or tax situation when and if you finally sell the property.

If you find yourself in either of the situations I mentioned—out of time or enjoying being a real estate investor—and want to sell the property, talk to your accountant, a real estate broker, or an exchange agent about the feasibility of using a 1031 Exchange.

CHAPTER TWELVE ACTION POINTS

☐ Familiarize yourself with the tax issues affecting your property both as your primary residence and as an investment.

☐ Find a good accountant; discuss all the tax issues related to your situation.

☐ Deductions are available to you as an investor/landlord that were not available to you as a homeowner.

☐ The tax issues with respect to renting property will affect your taxes right through the sale of the property.

☐ Make sure you're keeping all the records you need; separate them from your personal financial records. Discuss this with your accountant.

☐ Don't forget that depreciation and other deductions may be deductible from income other than the rental of your house.

☐ Keep the 1031 Exchange law in mind. You may be able to benefit from it.

Part Five

KEEP THE GOAL IN MIND: SELLING THE PROPERTY

MARKETING THE PROPERTY

Talk to Your Real Estate Agent

REMEMBER THAT IN most parts of the country there are two types of real estate agents: buyer's agents and seller's agents. If you've engaged an agent to sell your house, it will be a seller's agent. However since many agents will have access to the information about your house through the local multiple listing service, it is possible that some other agent may bring a buyer to see the property. This agent may be a buyer's agent and will be representing the interests of the buyer, not you. If you're working with a real estate agent to sell your property, it is generally wise to let him do most of the talking with prospective buyers and other agents.

If you have already given an agent the listing to sell your property, discuss your idea of leasing it before you go ahead with your plans. Use this part of the book to get the agent's opinions and ideas. The following are generalizations because I want you to be able to evaluate your agent's suggestions to your benefit.

Unless you are working with some type of fee-for-service agent, your agent will most likely not get paid until and unless he sells your house. Also you probably have signed a listing agreement giving your agent an exclusive right to sell your house for three months to one year. All of this is pretty typical.

As you think about renting your house, decide whether to continue marketing it while you rent it or to pull it off the market until things improve. I discussed the pros and cons of renting a house you're trying to sell in Chapter 1. Please reread that section and discuss these issues with your agent.

From the agent's point of view:

- He may be reluctant to spend time and money working the listing while the market is down.
- A rented house may be harder to sell since closing could be delayed until the tenant moves out.
- A rented house may be harder to show.
- He may worry that you'll like receiving income from the house and your motivation to sell may diminish.
- He will be concerned that the listing period will expire and you'll list the property with another agent.

These are valid and typical concerns all based on the idea that the agent earns his money by selling the property. Do not be surprised if your agent paints a very negative picture of your idea of renting the property, both from the perspective of making it more difficult to sell and the difficulties of being a landlord. Your agent may suggest lowering the price—probably not for the first time—before you rent the house in an attempt to sell it, or simply holding off for a little while "since the market seems to be improving."

Any and all of the suggestions your agent makes may be perfectly valid in your circumstances and under the market conditions in your area. Ultimately you're going to have to do your own research and make conclusions about the validity of your agent's suggestions.

Meanwhile, if you've gotten this far and have decided to rent your house, you lose nothing by having the agent continue to market the property while you rent it. However, it may be harder to get a tenant while you're still marketing the house unless you focus on short-term rentals.

Also discuss with your real estate agent the possibility of his acting as your rental agent and managing the property for you. Both topics are explained in Chapter 15.

Sell the House Yourself

Whether to sell your house yourself is a decision beyond the scope of this book, but it is an option. It will cost you time and money as you simultaneously follow the two tracks of renting and selling. Many of the concerns that a real estate agent would have will now be your concerns.

If you sell the house yourself, you save the commission that you would otherwise pay to an agent. It may allow you to sell the house at a cheaper price and therefore sooner. As a compromise, you may want to check out fee-for-service or limited-service brokers. These are agents who provide less-than-full real estate services at reduced fees.

Sell the House . . . Later

One possible action plan is to take the house off the market temporarily. The advantages of this are:

- You can focus on renting the property.
- You can offer a longer term lease to a tenant.
- If you are selling the house yourself, you can avoid wasting your time and money until the market improves.
- If the rent covers the bills, you lose nothing by waiting.

On the downside:

- You never know who will buy a house so you might miss THE buyer.
- If the rent doesn't cover the bills, the longer you rent the more money you lose.

What you do is ultimately your decision. However, whether or not you're using an agent or selling the house yourself, you will probably continue to market the house while you rent it. You or your agent may pull back somewhat on advertising, and focus on renting the property. Perhaps in six months or so or when the market begins to look better, you or your agent will get more aggressive with your marketing.

The remainder of this chapter will assume that whether or not you take a break from actively marketing the property, you will at some point market the property while it's occupied by a tenant.

A CONVERSATION TO AVOID

Conversation overheard between a tenant and a potential buyer of the property when neither the owner nor real estate agent was present.

BUYER: How is the neighborhood?
TENANT: Not bad; a little noisy though when the windows are open. I think we must be near a flight path for the airport.
BUYER: How about the schools? Are you happy with them?
TENANT: The schools are fine but not as good as where we used to live across town.
BUYER: You must be looking forward to moving then?
TENANT: No; not at all. The owner has been really nice. He's over here all the time fixing things. For a house this old he really takes good care of it.

Some version of this exchange has occurred more than once. Did the tenant mean to hurt the homeowner's chance to sell the property? Probably not. The moral: Don't leave a prospective buyer alone with the tenant. Ever!

Buyer Inspections

Potential buyers will want to see the house—perhaps more than once. This was easy when you were living in the house. Now there is an added step. Your tenant will have to be notified and a convenient time arranged for a potential buyer to look at the house.

Be sure that there is a clause in the lease that requires the tenant to permit you reasonable access to the property for buyer inspections. The problem may become your and the tenant's interpretation of "reasonable." You may have to deal with four issues with respect to buyer inspections and your tenants: notice, timing, frequency, and permission.

Notify the Tenant

Some tenants will want as much notice as possible before you bring someone to the house. They may want to be good tenants and cooperate with you by having the house in order. They may simply not like to be intruded upon without a certain amount of warning. Other tenants will not care about the condition of the premises since it's not their home, needing little or no time to clean up. Or they may simply be people who are very flexible in their lifestyle and have no objection to short-notice visits.

Whatever the type of tenant you have, never bring a buyer to the house without prior notice. You may have written into the lease that you can enter the house at any time not just in an emergency. Regardless, you should notify the tenants even if only to tell them that you're bringing a potential buyer to the house tomorrow morning while everyone is at work. It is common courtesy and good sense to allow the tenant to clean up, put things away, or otherwise prepare their home for a visit by their landlord and a stranger.

Finally, if you are using a real estate agent, discuss with the tenant the possibility that the agent will be making the appointment. Issues may arise as to who may be allowed to bring prospective buyers to the house, but the tenant cannot become the monitor of who is permitted to come to the house. It should simply be made clear that either you or your real estate agent will be the only person permitted to bring buyers to the house.

Timing

No time is convenient to have someone come through your home to inspect it. If your tenants tend to be out during the day on weekdays, this may be a convenient time for an inspection with a prospective buyer. This may not be convenient for your buyer; traditionally, inspections with buyers occur on weekends. Speak with your tenants during lease negotiations to set the ground rules for allowing prospective buyers to visit the property. Discuss the most convenient time for buyer inspections. Don't make any commitments to honor their requests, but indicate that you will try to provide plenty of notice and will attempt to honor their requests as to timing.

Place a clause in the lease to retain the right to conduct buyer inspections when no one is home. Tell the tenant they need not be home for a visit and that it would be better if they didn't make any plans around these appointments because last-minute cancellations are common.

Frequency

If enough visits occur while the tenants are home, they will become an inconvenience. Provided you give the tenants as much notice as possible and try to work with them with respect to scheduling, there is not much you can do to mitigate the inconvenience of frequent buyer inspections.

Permission

Overall permission to conduct buyer inspections should be established in the lease and during the lease negotiations. Tenants should not have the right to veto a prospective buyer inspection. If the tenant is hosting a major family event, you probably would not want to conduct the visit anyway. An occasional accommodation of the tenant's schedule is okay. But be careful not to ever ask the tenant's permission to visit the property.

You should say, "I'm bringing someone by to look at the property tomorrow at three o'clock." not "Is it okay if I bring someone by to look at the property tomorrow at three o'clock?" Let the tenant take the lead if the time or date is a problem.

Uncooperative Tenants

Be aware that you and your tenants may be working at cross purposes. Even short-term tenants want to stay in the house and leave on their own schedule, not yours. A tenant can sabotage a prospective sale in a number of ways. One way is to be extremely uncooperative about prospective buyer visits. Do not over-react to an occasional request to not bring a buyer to see the property. But if you sense a pattern developing, deal with it directly. When the tenant expresses reluctance at your bringing a buyer to the house, insist. It is your house. If you've made the appropriate arrangements in the lease and the tenant refuses to let you into the house, call your attorney and initiate eviction proceedings immediately.

Pre-buyer Inspections

Arrange to inspect the property before a prospective buyer visits. This may prove to be a double inconvenience to the tenant but it is a helpful step. You cannot do anything about any disarray, furniture placement, or general cleanliness or lack thereof by the tenant. The purpose of a pre-visit inspection is to determine if anything has occurred since your last visit that needs an explanation. Perhaps a window has been broken or a leaky pipe has left evidence of water damage. You may have time to deal with the issue, get something fixed, or clean up some damage. At least you will be prepared to offer an explanation to the real estate agent and/or the prospective buyer.

Be careful not to react to the conditions in which the tenant chooses to live. Provided the tenant is not damaging the property or causing an unsanitary condition that could lead to vermin or insect infestation, they are entitled to live the way they want to. You may feel that the house will not show that well because of clutter or sloppy housekeeping. This is one of the issues that you must accept when renting your property. Asking tenants to clean up or making disparaging remarks about their housekeeping will only engender resentment. And it is unlikely to get the house any cleaner.

Curb Appeal

Curb appeal is the impression a house makes as someone walks or drives by, and it remains a crucial component of selling a house. It is the first impression buyers get when they see the house. It tells the prospective buyer something about the attractiveness and condition of the inside of the house. Curb appeal may make the difference between buyers calling the number on the For Sale sign or continuing to drive by.

There's not much you can do that you haven't already done to the front of the house itself. The component that requires your ongoing attention is the lawn and garden maintenance. Keep a watchful eye on the outside of the house whenever you visit. If the tenant has agreed to maintain the lawn and they are not doing it to your standards, you may have to make other arrangements. An untidy lawn and front garden tells prospective buyers that they will find an untidy and ill-kept house on the inside. A buyer who drives by doesn't know that you've maintained the house meticulously and that it is your tenant who has let the lawn go uncut for weeks. First impressions do count. Make sure your house gives the right one.

Escort the Buyers at All Times

Do not permit prospective buyers to visit the house unescorted by either you or your real estate agent or a subagent working for your agent. Your real estate agent should never permit a buyer's agent (who represents the buyer) to escort a prospective buyer to the house unless your agent is present.

Avoid the possibility of any conversation between tenant and potential buyer that may have a negative impact on a possible sale. The prospective buyer may misunderstand a tenant's inadvertent remark. In some cases the tenant may purposely make remarks to discourage the buyer from making an offer or hurt your chances of selling the property.

There's no way to prevent a prospective buyer from coming back after an escorted visit and speaking to a tenant privately. It's wise to maintain a good relationship with tenants and ask them to refer all such visits to you.

If you are marketing the house yourself, you may decide to put a For Sale by Owner sign on the lawn. It should have a clearly visible phone number on the sign. Instruct tenants for their own safety never to permit an inspection of the house unless you are present.

Never Leave a Buyer Alone

This very specific warning is especially oriented toward those who will be marketing the house yourself. Security can be a major issue when prospective buyers visit a house. Rest assured that those earrings that belong to your tenant and went missing right after you brought someone to see the house will be blamed on the prospective buyer whom you may have left alone in a bedroom for a few minutes. This book is not designed to discuss the ins and outs of selling a house yourself. But since you could be held responsible for the security of your tenant's property, never leave the buyers alone in any part of the house when conducting an inspection.

Delivering the Property to the Buyer

Now that you have successfully sold your house, it's time to deliver it to the buyer. The lease may contain a termination-on sale-clause or provide for a month-to-month tenancy. Chapter 5 discussed the sequence of events and issues involving the tenant moving out. Picking up the sequence of events from the time the tenant has vacated the house, the next things to do are:

- Inspect the house and land.
- Repair any damage.
- Arrange for cleaning.
- Conduct a pre-closing inspection with the buyer.
- Close on the sale.

These steps are fairly obvious and will be familiar to those who have sold houses previously. I mention them because of the difference between selling a house you live in and selling a house you've rented out. After the tenants have moved out, it's important that you conduct a complete inspection of the property. Ideally this will be done with the tenants on the day they move out. Do this before returning their security deposit. In performing this inspection you're looking for damage the tenant might be responsible for and items of wear and tear that need to be fixed before you close on the property.

Items for which the tenant cannot be held responsible might include leaky faucets, stopped-up drains, nonfunctioning appliances, and wear and tear to the house in general. You'll want to fix these things before you conduct the closing inspection on the property. While the property clearly does not need to be in brand-new condition, you want to avoid the possibility of a delay in the closing because of something the buyer wants fixed or cleaned. If you're working with a real estate agent, consult with him or her about what repairs to undertake before spending inordinate amounts of money.

The general standard for delivery of a house for closing a sale is broom-clean. This may mean nothing more than vacuum-cleaning the house and mopping a few floors. It could also mean an entire weekend spent cleaning, or hiring a professional cleaning service.

CHAPTER THIRTEEN ACTION POINTS

☐ Consult with your real estate agent about the issues of marketing your property while renting it.

☐ Consider pulling your property off the market completely until the market improves.

☐ Make sure you've retained the right to take prospective buyers on inspections of the house even if the tenants are not home.

☐ Always notify the tenants that you or your real estate agent will bring someone to see the house.

☐ Never let a prospective buyer tour the house unescorted and never leave them alone in the house.

☐ Never give the tenant the right to tell you that you can't bring a prospective buyer (or future renter) to see the house.

☐ Try to inspect the house yourself before bringing a prospective buyer.

- [ ] Continually monitor the curb appeal of the house and property.

- [ ] Make sure the tenants understand that they are not to allow people to tour the house unless escorted by you or your real estate agent.

- [ ] If you're using a real estate agent, make sure you understand who is representing you and who might be representing the buyer.

- [ ] When you have a contract for sale of the house and the tenant moves out, conduct a compete inspection of the house and grounds. Make all repairs and arrange for the house to be cleaned in preparation for the pre-closing walk-through inspection by the buyer.

CHAPTER FOURTEEN

LEASE WITH AN OPTION TO BUY

Contracts and Options

A CONTRACT IS simply an exchange of promises between two people. Depending on what is being contracted, a contract may run for many pages with details and terms and conditions. When you sign the contract of sale for your house, you promise to sell your house to someone and the buyer promises to buy the house from you. The point of the exchange of promises in this type of contract is that each of you can force the other to abide by the terms of the contract. Legally, you both must act to fulfill the promises that you made.

An option is a little different from the contract just described. In an option agreement, only one person can be forced to act.

Say you're a builder and you find some land that you might want to build on. The land is for sale but you don't have all the pieces in place like the financing and plans to build. You need more time but meanwhile you don't want to lose the land. You don't want to buy the land outright because if you don't get the financing and approvals, you don't want to be stuck with a piece of property that you can't use. The solution to this problem, if the owner agrees, is an option agreement.

For a certain amount of money the owner agrees to take the land off the market and give you the right to buy it at a price that you've already agreed to in the option agreement. You and the owner also agree on the term of the agreement. So the option might read that for the sum of $5,000, you have an option for one year to buy the land at $100,000. What does this mean exactly for you and the landowner?

Anytime during that one-year time period you can "exercise your option" and force the landowner to sell you the property for $100,000. Even if the property has increased in value, you can still force the sale at the $100,000 price. Conversely the landowner cannot force you to buy. So if the value of the land went down significantly, unlike a normal sales contract, he or she could not force you to purchase the property. Unlike a regular sales contract where both parties must act, in an option only one party must act. The other party has the option to act or not.

Lease with an Option to Buy

The lease with an option to buy combines two elements: the lease and the option. You are giving your tenant an option to buy the property. In most cases the lease and the option are negotiated at the same time. However, a regular tenant without an option can request an option at a later date. This tenant might become interested in purchasing the property but may have to settle some other business matters before being able to buy it. They know you are marketing the property and do not wish to lose it but are simply not ready yet to make you a firm offer and sign a purchase contract.

A lease agreement with an option to buy can be attractive for a tenant as well as the owner. It can also reduce your flexibility in selling the property. Address the following issues in a lease agreement with an option to purchase:

- Term
- Charge for the option
- Property price
- Credit for rent
- Assignment of the option

tip

A "LEASE WITH OPTION TO PURCHASE" CONVERSATION

TENANT: Yes, I would like to rent your house. I wish we could buy it, but we don't have enough for the down payment right now.

OWNER: Suppose I gave you credit from the rent toward a down payment? We'd first agree on a price. Each month I'd set aside a portion of your rent toward a down payment on the house. If you decided to buy the house, the portion of each month's rent would be credited toward the down payment.

TENANT: Suppose I didn't buy the house? Would I get any of that money back?

OWNER: No, it would be just part of the rent.

TENANT: Suppose someone else wanted to buy the house in the meantime?

OWNER: If I had a buyer for the house and you had not exercised your option to buy, I'd have to sell. I really couldn't hold it.

TENANT: How much of the rent would you be willing to credit toward the down payment?

OWNER: If you're really interested in this, why don't we discuss the price of the house first and go from there.

Term of the Option

It may seem that the obvious thing to do is to set the term of the option as the same term as the lease. However, there is nothing to say that you must or even that it's a good idea. Remember that the option requires you to take the property off the market for the term of the option. The option can be the same or shorter than the lease. It can also be set for some other period of time if the lease is month to month.

The term of the option is completely arbitrary and relates to the market conditions and your plans for marketing the property. If you are not going to actively market the property for a year, you lose nothing by giving the tenant a one-year option. The same applies if you believe the market will not improve enough for a year or two to sell the house at the price you want. On the other hand, if you are going to actively market the property, you may grant a short one, say six months, or none.

An option to purchase may be a lease sweetener for tenants who need to get their financial situation in order before buying a house. They may be newcomers to the area and need to sell their previous home first. As you can see there is no one right answer for the option term.

You may set a shorter option term with the possibility of renewal. Say you and your tenant agree to a one-year lease and they want a one-year purchase option. You can initially agree to a six-month option and indicate that you would be willing to discuss an extension of the option at that point depending on market conditions. The initial period could even be shorter, say three or four months, if you believe the market is going to change soon and you want to retain some flexibility in your marketing plans.

Another possibility is to keep the property on the market but still give the tenant an option to purchase. The benefit to the tenant would likely be a provision to provide some credit toward the purchase price from the rent paid. This aspect of an option will be discussed later in this chapter.

Charge for the Option

You should not try to charge for an option. This is not a conventional option situation. The tenants are already paying you rent. And they may feel that if they exercise a purchase option they're making your life easier by not having to market the property further. If you believe the market will turn soon and that an option has real value to the tenant and is an inconvenience to you, there are alternatives:

- Don't offer the option in the first place.
- Decline to give the option if the tenant brings it up.
- Keep the option period as short as possible, say three or four months.

Set the Property Price Now

An option to purchase includes either a firm price for the purchase or an agreed-to method for setting the price at a later date. If neither of these is in the agreement, the option is more of a right of first refusal than a true option. Right of first refusal is discussed at the end of this chapter.

Agreeing on a purchase price in the option agreement is the most straightforward thing to do. Pricing the house for sale is not a subject for this book; however, consider the following:

- The most probable price for which the house would currently sell
- The price you've been asking at which the house hasn't sold
- The price you want or need to sell the house for
- The price that the house might sell for at the end of the option period

There is also nothing that says you need to negotiate the price. You can set the price and offer the option at that price on a "take it or leave it" basis. If you decide to include the price in the option, that will be the price you'll get for the house if the tenant exercises the option, even if the market improves significantly during the option period.

Set the Property Price Later

Another way to set the purchase price in an option is not to actually agree to a dollar amount but to agree to a method to set the price when and if the option is exercised. The most logical way is to engage a professional appraiser. Since many people assume that appraisers will favor the person who hired them, you might agree to the average of two appraisals: one by someone you engaged and one by someone whom the tenant contracted.

The danger of this approach may be obvious. If the tenant has access to an unscrupulous appraiser who comes in with an extremely low value for the house, even the average of two appraisals could result in an unusually low selling price. An alternative to this is to agree ahead of time on two appraisers that are acceptable to both of you, though this may still not mitigate the issue of the potentially unfavorable appraisal.

Agreeing to a methodology to set the future price is complicated and uncertain. On the positive side, you stand a better chance of getting market value for the property. On the other hand, because of the way an option is structured you might have to sell the house at market value, which could be less than you want to sell it for. Agreeing to a way to set the price in the future is not the best approach to the option to buy.

Credit for Rent

Perhaps the stickiest issue to negotiate on a lease with an option to buy is whether or not to give credit to the tenant for rent paid. Market conditions are the primary factor in either offering this or agreeing to it if the tenant asks. We've assumed that the market for sales is not favorable, or you would not be considering renting your house.

You are renting the house and expect to be paid rent. The option agreement is an extra as far as you're concerned. The tenants view it almost as an installment purchase plan, and expect to receive full credit for the rent paid if they decide to purchase your property.

If you agree to a relatively high price, it may be that giving the tenant full or partial credit for their rent toward the purchase price makes sense. Alternatively, the rental market as well as the sales market may not be good and you need to sweeten the pot to get a tenant. In that case, some credit for the rent may be necessary even if the agreed-to price is not as high as you wish.

Optimally, from your perspective, you don't want to give any credit. If the tenant asks, you may have to negotiate it. If there is a purchase option agreed to but no credit for rent, it is probably wise to place a clause in the lease and option agreement that no credit is being granted for the rent paid toward the purchase price. This should also be explained to the tenant. Check with your attorney about proper wording of the option agreement and any other language associated with the option and rent credit.

Remember that credit for the rent toward purchase will kick in only if the tenant buys the house. If they do buy the house, the rent you've received will be less than you expected. Refer to Chapter 19 for math examples of this.

Use the Option as a Sweetener

If market conditions are such that both the rental and sales markets are slow, you may need to do something to attract renter attention. If you've decided that you can live with an option to buy, you may want to place this in your tenant advertisement. Language such as "Option to purchase available" is sufficient to set your house apart and may attract a tenant who is also a potential buyer. If after a fair amount of advertising you have no prospective tenants and if it fits into your financial plan, you could advertise "Partial credit given toward purchase price from rent" or "Portion of rent will be applied to purchase price." This is recommended as a last resort, but it might be worth trying this approach before lowering the rent. If you got a tenant with the option and credit-for-rent agreement, there's always a chance they won't buy the house—in which case you have received the higher rent.

Brokers and Options

If you are renting your house and have negotiated an option agreement that is subsequently exercised resulting in the sale of your house, and you did all of this without the help of a real estate broker, then you should not have to pay a fee to the broker. However, you may be legally obligated to do so, depending on the agreement in place at the time of the sale or at the time the option was signed.

If an Exclusive Right to Sell listing agreement was in place with your broker at the time you leased the property and signed the option-to-purchase agreement, the broker may be able to enforce a fee payment. Remember that an Exclusive Right to Sell listing agreement entitles the broker to a fee/commission no matter who ultimately sells the property even if that's you or another broker.

Suppose you've been trying to sell the house yourself and at the time you sign the lease and the option agreement there is no listing agreement in place. Further suppose that you decide to engage the services of a real estate broker while the house is rented and the option agreement is in effect. Will you owe a fee to your broker if the tenant exercises the option to purchase the house while the listing agreement is in effect? If you signed an Exclusive Right to Sell listing agreement, the answer is "possibly."

Assuming that a broker was not involved in renting the house and negotiating the option agreement, how can you protect yourself from paying your broker a fee if your tenant decides to buy the house—or in fact if any tenant you find yourself decides to buy the house, with or without an option agreement? There are two ways.

The first is to sign an Exclusive Agency listing agreement instead of an Exclusive Right to Sell agreement. The Exclusive Agency agreement allows you to sell the house yourself without paying a commission. The alternative is to specifically exclude from the Exclusive Right to Sell agreement—either in general or by name—any tenant who exercises their option to buy the property. Do not allow the real estate broker to put a time limit on this exclusion. Assuming that the real estate broker is not assisting you in finding a tenant or negotiating the option, the Exclusive Right to Sell listing agreement should exclude the following:

- Current tenants exercising a right-to-purchase option
- Future tenants with whom an option agreement is negotiated
- Future option agreements
- Any and all tenants you find yourself who may purchase the house

Have your attorney check the wording in the agreement with your broker.

The Tenant Wants a Right of First Refusal

A right of first refusal is exactly what its name implies. Before you can sell your house, you would have to offer the tenant the right to buy the house at the same price as a bona fide offer. Tenants like to negotiate a right of first refusal as a way to protect their future interest without committing themselves to purchasing a property at a specific price.

The benefit of the right of first refusal tends to be to the person who holds the right—in this case, the tenant. There is no real benefit to you. If anything, it can be a detriment when it comes time to sell. Any bona fide offer, usually backed up by a contract or a written offer to purchase, would have to be presented to the tenant. The tenant would have a certain amount of time to match the offer or decline it. This would delay the sale and in a tight market could turn off a buyer. Furthermore, if the tenant agrees to the offer and you cancel the contract with the original buyer and then the tenant fails to secure financing, you lose the buyer. And the right of first refusal is still in place for the next offer that comes along. You should not offer rights of first refusal.

CHAPTER FOURTEEN ACTION POINTS

☐ Consider an option to purchase when renting the property.

☐ Beware of tying up the property with an overly long option to purchase.

☐ Set the property price in the option, if possible.

☐ Use the option and possible rent credit as a lure for potential tenants when advertising the property in a poor rental market.

☐ Take necessary steps to avoid paying a real estate brokerage fee or commission if you sell the house yourself to a tenant.

☐ Don't offer the tenant a right of first refusal.

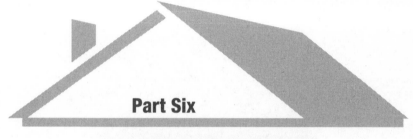

Part Six

PROFESSIONAL PROPERTY MANAGEMENT

CHAPTER FIFTEEN

USE A PROFESSIONAL PROPERTY MANAGER

AT THIS POINT you've decided to rent your house while you wait for the market to change so you can sell it. You may be moving some distance from your old house or you may be too busy to manage the property yourself. Maybe you've read through most of this book and are not that interested in the day-to-day job of being a landlord. Or maybe you just want to consider the professional property management option.

An Informed Choice
You should have a good idea of what it takes to manage a rental property. Now that you understand the work involved, you can make a more informed decision whether to self-manage the property or hire a professional. As you'll see there are a number of issues to consider, including finding the right person and negotiating an appropriate agreement.

Pros of using a professional property manager
- The property is too far away for you to reasonably manage yourself.
- You don't have the time to devote to managing a rental property.
- You would do some of the simpler tasks involved in managing a rental property, but you don't want to deal with broken furnaces in the middle of the night or obnoxious tenants.

- You do not believe you have the knowledge, even with the help of this book, to adequately manage the property.
- You simply don't want to deal with the day-to-day issues of being a landlord.
- A professional may be able to manage the property better and more efficiently than you can.

Cons of using a professional property manager
- You will have to find a property manager.
- You may not be able to find a professional to manage just one single-family rental property on a short-term basis.
- It will cost you money.
- The property may not generate enough in rent to pay all the bills and pay for a property manager.
- You may not want to give up control of the property.
- If you hire a property manager, you'll lose the opportunity to see what it's like to actually manage an investment property. This is a golden opportunity to see if you like being a landlord, which could lead to becoming a real estate investor.

Every Broker Is Not a Property Manager
A real estate broker's license is the basic legal requirement for becoming a property manager in most places. However, keep in mind that not every real estate broker has the knowledge, skills, or temperament to be a property manager. Brokers receive general training in various aspects of real estate law and procedures. In some states they may also receive training in investment properties and property management. The primary training and experience of most real estate brokers, however, is in sales. The pros and cons of using your real estate broker as a property manager will be discussed later, but for now keep in mind that while most property managers are brokers, not all brokers are property managers.

Property Management Credentials

Property managers generally must have a real estate broker's license in order to be property managers. While broker training and experience requirements vary, many states require at least some course work in property management in order to receive a real estate broker's license. But property management is considered a specialized field of real estate. The National Association of Realtors through its Institute for Real Estate Management offers training and information for property managers. It offers the Certified Property Manager (CPM) designation indicating that the designee has, through study and experience, achieved a certain level of expertise in the field of property management. Ideally you should be looking for someone with this credential.

Find a Professional Manager

Once you have decided to use a professional property manager, you need to locate one. Ask for referrals from real estate brokers or attorneys, and refer to the Institute for Real Estate Management's website *www.irem.com* for more information. Search the Internet, yellow pages, your local chamber of commerce, and property management company signs posted on buildings.

Remember that you are looking for a professional property manager; that is, someone whose primary or sole business is managing property for other people. Although there are some managers who manage single-family houses, many specialize in the larger residential and nonresidential types of investment properties found in and around metropolitan areas. If your property is located in an outer-ring suburb, you may have difficulty locating a professional manager for your property. You may also have difficulty finding a professional to manage a single house for a short period of time. But don't be discouraged. Keep looking and consider other possibilities, including talking to real estate brokers who may want to manage property as part of their real estate business.

Select a Property Manager

Once you've identified several property managers, contact them, discuss your situation, and ask for a written proposal. The proposal can be fairly simple, but it should include the duties they will perform for you, the fee they will charge, and the term of the agreement that they expect. As with any proposal that you might solicit, it is helpful to be able to compare apples to apples so it's a good idea to detail the expectations that you have of the property manager. In this way they can "bid" on the same work and you can make a valid comparison. Ask for and check on their references. Try to get references that relate to other small properties like one- and two-family houses that they have previously or are currently managing. A reference from the owner of a shopping mall may be impressive, but it doesn't tell you how much attention they will pay to a relatively small property like yours.

Above all, don't be afraid to ask a lot of questions. Your choice of a property manager should be based not only on how knowledgeable a prospective manager is, but also on his willingness to explain things to you. Remember that this is the person you'll be working with and who will have to maintain good relations with your tenant.

Pros of using your broker as your property manager

- The broker is already there, so you won't have to search for anyone.
- You may have a difficult time finding a professional property manager to manage the property on a temporary basis.
- If your broker can't or won't manage the property, maybe someone at her company will.
- The broker knows the property.
- The broker usually knows the market area and often has knowledge of the rental market.
- The broker has a vested interest in keeping you happy since she wants to ultimately sell your house.

- Since the broker wants to sell the house, she will take extra care to see that the property remains in good condition.
- The broker may be willing to manage the property at a more favorable fee than a professional manager, since the broker ultimately will collect a fee for selling the property.

Cons of using your broker as your property manager
- Your broker may have no training or experience in property management.
- The broker's primary job is to sell houses. Management would be a part-time effort at best.
- Once the broker is making a regular fee for managing the property, his incentive to sell it may diminish. This is probably not realistic since he will likely make a bigger, faster paycheck by selling the property than by managing it. The thought is worth consideration, however.
- While there should be no conflict between management decisions and marketing decisions, in the event there were, you could get possibly conflicting advice from the same person.

Have a Friend or Relative Manage the Property
The question of whether or not to engage a friend or relative to manage the property may be inevitable. You are moving quite a distance away and having trouble finding a professional manager. Coincidentally, you have a trusted friend or relative who is available and interested in the job. Reconsider this if you do not wish to share confidential information with this person. This person may have no property management experience and be unprepared to assume the legal liability involved. It is hard to fire a friend or relative.

On the other hand, the right friend or family member may be the most trustworthy person you can find, and he or she may be willing to do the job at a reduced fee. Caution should prevail, however, in making this choice. Business and friendship or family usually don't mix.

One other thought about hiring a relative as the property manager: If you have grown children who have any interest, managing the property under your general supervision could be a wonderful experience. It would give them a taste of what it is to be a landlord and might spark an interest for investing in real estate later on. The first step is to have them read this book and see what they think of the idea. And oh yes, don't be cheap. Pay them a fee for taking this on.

tip **THE PRICE OF ABSENCE TIMES TWO**
Joan was encouraged by a family member to buy a small multifamily building in a city about four hours from where she lived. The neighborhood was stable and served a number of local medical and law schools and hospitals. She hired a local real estate agent to manage the property. The property was just far enough away to make it inconvenient for Joan to visit. Within five years Joan was surprised to learn that the neighborhood had completely changed and the building was not worth what she had paid for it.

You can create your own moral from this story. Should Joan have visited the property regularly? Should she have stipulated in the management agreement that the agent should report on any significant changes in the neighborhood that would affect the value of the property?

The real moral of the story is that no one will take care of your property as you would and the expectations of hiring a professional manager must be tempered by your continuing attention to the property.

What Are You Trying to Accomplish?

Regardless of whether you hire a professional property manager, your broker, or your cousin, have a clear idea of what you want to accomplish in managing the property and convey that to the manager. This book assumes that renting the property is a temporary detour on the road to eventually selling it. There are questions to address in your own mind as well as discuss with the manager.

- For how long do you want to rent the property?
- Is this time frame based on some arbitrary period like one year or two, or based on some level of recovery in the real estate market?
- Will you continue to market the property or take it off the market while it is being rented?

Do some calculations based on potential sale price versus rental income versus carrying costs on the new home in order to make a rational decision about when to sell the property.

CHAPTER FIFTEEN ACTION POINTS

☐ Decide if professional property management is your best course of action.

☐ Make sure your broker has the proper experience if you choose him or her to manage the property.

☐ Check out the credentials of any potential manager.

☐ Be aware that you may have difficulty finding a professional manager to manage one house.

☐ Be careful of using a friend or relative to manage the property.

PROPERTY MANAGEMENT AGREEMENT

ALTHOUGH YOU OWN a single-family house and not a large office building, the basis of your relationship with a property manager is the property management agreement. It should set forth in writing the duties, responsibilities, and expectations each of you has of the other. While it need not be overly complicated, it should not be taken lightly. As with any contract, principal issues should be agreed to and it should be drafted by or at least reviewed by your attorney.

A contract has no force in and of itself. A contract expresses the promises made between two people. Its force is that it forms the basis for legal action if one or the other person does not fulfill contractual obligations. It is therefore important that these obligations be spelled out as much as possible.

It seems to be universally true that unresolved contractual issues will be presumed to be resolved at a later date in favor of the party doing the presuming. That means both parties think they are going to get the benefit of an unresolved issue. Since that is almost impossible, as many issues as possible should be resolved in the agreement.

Following is a brief discussion of the important items that should be included in a property management agreement.

Term

You'll have to agree on a term for the property management agreement. A typical agreement will last for at least a year so that the manager can recoup his initial costs. Yours is not a typical situation, however. If the real estate market improves dramatically, you may wish to sell the property immediately. If you are going to continue marketing the property while it is being rented, you'll want to be able to sell any time you have a suitable buyer.

The property manager should realize that this is a temporary arrangement and incur few costs in setting up a rent collection system or developing an operating or capital budget.

A month-to-month term, such that you or the manager can terminate on one month's notice, is best. It is unlikely that the manager will terminate the agreement and you want the flexibility of being able to sell the property quickly.

Management Fee—Possibilities

Property management fees are negotiable. In the world of professional investors and property managers, fees are set one of four ways:

1. Flat fee
2. Percentage of gross or net income
3. Leasing fees
4. A combination of any two or three of these options

The percentage fee and the lease fee are designed to reward the property manager for good performance. The more rent the manager collects and the faster she rents the space the more money she makes.

Though you hope you will have one tenant who will remain in the house for as long as you're renting it, here are a few considerations in determining the fee arrangement.

- The property will have to be looked after even during periods of vacancy.
- Finding a tenant, negotiating a lease, and moving a new tenant in require work for which the property manager will wish to be paid.

■ The fee should be an incentive to the manager to do a good job while not being a financial burden to the property.

Management Fee—Professional Manager

A professional property manager may very well want his standard fee for managing the property. This will most likely be a percentage of the rent. Your negotiating position on this will be to point out that there will be very little for the manager to do except for collecting the rent and paying a few bills. The usual duties of managing a large rental complex will be considerably reduced and therefore a lower percentage should be charged. If you need to sweeten the pot, you might offer an incentive of a flat fee every time the manager has to negotiate a new lease.

Management fee—your broker

If you decide to use your broker as your property manager, you might be able to negotiate a more favorable fee arrangement. Your broker wants to keep you happy because she ultimately wants to sell your house and make a larger fee.

Consider paying your broker a fee that will be deducted in whole or in part from the fee paid when she sells your property. To some extent this will "marry" you to the broker, since if you switch brokers you'll end up paying the management fee and the brokerage fee. On the other hand, it is a good deal for your broker since she will make some money either way. If the broker is reluctant to give you credit for the full fee, you might be able to negotiate some other arrangement to receive at least partial credit for the management fee against the sales commission.

Management fee—friend or relative

There is never an easy or right way to negotiate fees with a relative or friend. You may not wish to pay the nonprofessional the same as a professional, but you expect him to perform the same duties as the professional. If you expect him to do it all, then why wouldn't you pay him as you would a professional? Perhaps because you don't expect him to be as competent as a professional would be. In which case, you have to ask yourself why you are hiring him to manage the property. Whatever agreement you negotiate, do your best to treat it like a business arrangement and not as a favor.

Management fee—negotiation

As with any service or project related to real estate, it's a good idea to obtain several bids or proposals. The same holds true for hiring a property manager. You should obtain at least three bids for the services of a manager. Make sure in obtaining and reviewing the proposals that you are comparing the same services. Unless you've already made up your mind to keep some of the responsibilities yourself, it's a good idea to solicit proposals to perform all property management duties, including obtaining tenants. (See the later section, Decide How Much You Want to Do.) Obtain full-service bids and then negotiate for a reduced fee if you want to do any of the work yourself.

tip **ONE FROM COLUMN A . . . ONE FROM COLUMN B . . .**

A.	B.	C.
Professional manager	Percentage of gross rent	Maintenance
Broker	Flat fee	Rent collection
Friend or relative	Leasing fee	Bill paying
Combination	Leasing	Combination

Put together your management agreement with these important choices as your basis.

Termination

The time to negotiate the conditions under which a contract can be terminated is always at the beginning of the contractual relationship. When the agreement has to be terminated, it may be too late to have a reasonable discussion.

Termination for Cause

This is always appropriate as a way to terminate the contract if the manager is not fulfilling his or her duties. A professional manager may require that the disagreement be submitted to arbitration rather than going to court. If possible, avoid the termination-for-cause section altogether. Instead, simply have a termination clause that suits your needs, which should be termination without cause on reasonable notice, say sixty days. If the manager agrees to this, you will not need to prove any reasons to terminate the contract if you're unhappy with the manager or simply want to assume the management duties yourself. Most likely, you will want to terminate the agreement on relatively short notice anyway since your primary goal is to sell the property. A clause simply stating that either party can terminate the agreement on thirty or sixty days' notice should be sufficient. The manager may wish some type of severance—for example, one or more months' compensation after the termination date. Since this is clearly a temporary arrangement from the outset, resist this. If you believe it is justified, it should be easy to agree on the severance being the monthly fee times a certain number of months.

Manager's Duties

The property manager's duties should be clearly stated and may include anything the manager agrees to. Typical duties would be rent collection, payment of bills, maintenance of the property, periodic property inspection, responding to tenant complaints and concerns, finding new tenants as needed, lease negotiations, and reporting to you on a regular basis. You may wish to fine-tune this list of duties. For example, you will probably want to continue paying the mortgage, taxes, and insurance yourself. Maintenance duties should be detailed since many single-family home leases call for the tenants to do routine maintenance such as snow removal and lawn mowing. Some or all utility bills might be paid for by the tenant. Be as specific as you can as to exactly what is expected of the property manager.

Manager's Authority—General

This section of the agreement will deal with what you will authorize the manager to do without checking with you first. Typical considerations revolve around repairs and maintenance, handling the finances, and leasing activities.

Manager's Authority—Maintenance and Repairs

Can the manager call the plumber to repair a leaky faucet or have the furnace repaired without your approval? If so, can the manager have the furnace replaced if needed, without your approval? The most reasonable arrangement is for the manager to have the authority on his or her own to authorize repairs up to a certain amount of money. Capital repairs—that is, large items like replacing a roof or a furnace—should require your specific approval before the manager can proceed. The manager's job should be to gather information and costs from several contractors and present it with a recommendation to you for a decision.

Manager's Authority—Finances

The property manager should have basic control of the property's finances (i.e., collect the rent, deposit it in an account, and pay the bills). You and the manager should determine which bills will be paid routinely from the rent, which bills—such as the mortgage—will be paid by you, and how much money—if any—will be sent to you each month. A further consideration would be any costs that the manager would bear out of his own funds. For example, if you are going to pay the manager a bonus for leasing the property, see if the manager will pay some or all of the associated advertising. Another thing to consider is an upper dollar limit on what the manager can spend. To some extent, this can be related to authorizing repairs. For example, you might permit the manager to spend $200 on any single repair bill but require specific approval for any expenditure over that. Your trust in the manager's ability and experience and your own experience with the property should guide your decision on this issue.

Owner's Responsibility

If the property manager's responsibilities can be viewed as a partially filled glass, the owner's responsibility is what will fill the remainder of the glass. The more the manager does, the less the owner has to do and vice versa. For example, the owner may want to retain direct responsibility for obtaining tenants and negotiating the lease terms including the rent. On the other hand, the owner may want the property manager to do all the work of finding the tenant and negotiating the lease but will retain final approval of the lease. The owner may wish to retain the responsibility of paying the mortgage and/or taxes and property insurance and have the property manager take care of all the other bills.

Decide How Much You Want to Do

There is no standard, one size fits all, balance between owner responsibility and authority and manager responsibility and authority. As an owner, consider factors similar to those you think about when making a decision whether to hire a professional manager or manage the property yourself.

- How much time do you realistically have to devote to managing the property?
- Are you psychologically equipped to deal with landlord/tenant issues?
- Do you tend to be someone who can delegate responsibility or are you more hands-on?
- How close to the property will you be living?
- Are there things you want to keep confidential from the manager, such as the amount of the mortgage payment?
- Will the manager reduce the management fee to reflect any responsibilities that you assume?

Communication and Reporting

The frequency and content of periodic reports from the manager should be clearly stated in the property management agreement.

A typical reporting period is monthly with the report containing financial information as well as items of interest to the owner, such as repairs, maintenance, and lease terminations and renewals. In the straightforward management of a single-family house, a quarterly report may be adequate. The manager will also need to produce an annual report appropriate for use in preparing your tax returns. Do not agree to a management proposal where the only report the manager submits is an annual report. Things can get out of hand far too quickly for you to be uninformed for a year. If you are not living nearby, you will also want the manager to report on changing market conditions in the neighborhood. The manager should also be willing to provide you with several phone numbers and an e-mail address where she can be contacted.

Property Inspection

Normally property managers will inspect the property and offer suggestions toward making the property more marketable as a rental. You should follow their recommendations for complying with safety and building codes and reducing existing liability issues. When discussing recommendations for cosmetic and maintenance work to increase the rentability of the property, consider the following factors:

- What is the item cost versus its impact on making the property more rentable?
- Can the cost of the item be recouped through charging a higher rent?
- Will the item take a long time to complete, effectively delaying rental of the property?
- Will the item enhance the ultimate salability of the property (i.e., how quickly the property will sell)?
- Will the cost of the item result in a higher sale price of the property?

Budgeting

As the property manager inspects the property she will form an impression of how rentable the property is and what rent might be charged. To work out a budget for managing the property, provide the manager with a history of bills going back at least a year. Approval of the final budget will be up to you, but be aware that there is not a great deal of flexibility in a budget when renting a single-family house. Part of the budget approval process will be to determine if you will absorb any costs, such as the mortgage. If it appears that the property generates a negative cash flow, you will have to commit to either paying some of the bills directly or periodically depositing money into an account accessible to the property manager and maintaining a certain level of funds in that account.

Insurance

Property managers should carry insurance to pay for any liability that may result from their error. In addition, they should be willing to indemnify you against any liability that occurs as a result of their management actions. Simply stated, the property manager should pay for any personal injuries or property damages that may occur as a result of the manager's wrongdoing. You do not want to be responsible for the manager's actions while acting as your agent (though you could still be sued). Have your attorney review this element of the agreement carefully.

Some Final Thoughts

Managing a one-family home may not be a high priority for many professional property managers, especially if they know it's only a temporary job. However, it's a high priority for you. Your property is not a million-square-foot shopping mall, but the manager should be willing to commit to certain duties and responsibilities and then follow through with attention and commitment.

I do not believe the agreement to manage a one-family house should be any less formal than that of managing a much larger building. It ultimately may be less detailed and complex, but all the major elements of a standard agreement should be considered.

Hiring a professional to manage your property can relieve you of a burden of time and detail while you wait to sell your property. It does not, however, relieve you of responsibility for your property. You're still likely to make certain decisions, including hiring the property manager in the first place. It also does not relieve you of paying attention to the property and the neighborhood and market conditions. After all, your ultimate goal is to sell the property. I've known investors who could have saved themselves some money by selling sooner than they'd planned because the neighborhood property values were declining and they didn't know it. You can periodically discuss this with your manager, but there is no substitute for an occasional visit to the property if it is at all practical.

CHAPTER SIXTEEN ACTION POINTS

☐ A flat fee makes the most sense for a simple house rental management.

☐ Treat the management arrangement professionally and have a written agreement.

☐ Use the leverage of the future sale to negotiate a better fee if you use your broker.

☐ If you are living far away from your house, be sure to get periodic reports about what's happening in the neighborhood.

☐ Make sure the manager understands that your ultimate intention is to sell the house.

☐ Be clear in the agreement as to the manager's duties and authority.

Part Seven

RENT FOR PROFIT

CHAPTER SEVENTEEN

RENT A ROOM IN YOUR HOUSE

IF YOU ARE not ready to make the leap into renting your house while you wait to sell it, renting out one or two rooms may be a good compromise. There are a number of things to think about in deciding to do this.

Keep It Legal

Renting out a room in one's own home is usually not covered by local zoning laws. Local municipalities are generally concerned about single-family houses becoming illegal rooming houses where several rooms are rented to different people. Usually, there are also zoning controls regarding turning a one-family house into a two-family house even if only by renting out existing space, such as a basement, as a complete apartment without making any physical changes to the space.

The distinction that is usually made between a room and an apartment is the existence of a kitchen in the apartment. Renting out a spare bedroom is generally not a problem. Renting out a finished basement that happens to have a kitchen is usually illegal in single-family-zoned areas.

Zoning and building ordinances are administered at the municipal level so they vary throughout the country. Visit your local building and/or zoning office and discuss with the officials how you can legally rent space in your house. Under certain circumstances, say if the tenant were a family member, you may get permission to rent that finished basement with a kitchen. Always check the legality of your plans for renting space in your house before proceeding further. And don't forget when checking with the municipal officials to find out about any physical or structural requirements for the room you're renting out.

The remainder of this chapter will be concerned with renting a spare room rather than a completely finished basement with a kitchen.

Privacy

Arguably, privacy and security are the two most prevalent reasons people don't rent a room in their house.

Some people require a level of privacy that would make renting a room in their house impossible. Others may actually like the idea of having a "roommate." You might be somewhere in between. First, you'll need to decide where you are on the privacy continuum.

Next, you should examine your house for room rental possibilities. You may have to compromise on privacy depending on how the rental space is configured, where it is in the house, how your tenant will get to it, and what other facilities the tenant will use.

Security—Picking the Right Renter

A lack of privacy can be annoying. A lack of security can keep you awake at night or be dangerous. You're going to have a stranger living in your house and the physical arrangement of the space you're renting can play a part in providing some security.

You can increase your security by not renting to a stranger; perhaps a family member or friend needs a place to stay for a while.

The next best thing to knowing the person you're renting to or knowing someone who knows them is obtaining and checking references. This is a crucial step that should not be bypassed no matter how nice the person seems. Any prospective renter should be able to provide the names of at least three nonfamily personal references. Call these references and ask how long they've known your prospective renter, the nature of their relationship, and their opinion of the renter.

In addition to personal references, you'll want the important business reference that will verify employment or other source of income. You'll need the name of employer, length of time employed, a pay statement within the last month, and a name and phone number to verify employment.

The prospective renter should provide to you a current address, and a previous one (if the current address is less than two years), and a phone number.

At this point, see if the local police station will do a criminal check on the prospective renter. You'll also want to check the sex offender list. Taking these steps will give you some sense of security about your selection of a tenant.

Security—Living with a Renter

You've done the best you can to check out the person to whom you're going to rent a room. But the physical arrangement in the house is such that you will be sharing each other's space to some extent. Although you feel secure personally, standard security measures and common sense should still guide your actions. A few tips to remember:

- Lock up your valuables and any private items when you're not home.
- Don't leave cash, jewelry, or personal papers lying around.
- Vary your schedule if you can.
- Don't always tell your renter what time you'll be at home.
- Strictly enforce any off-limit rules that you may establish.

Find the Space to Rent

The idea of renting a room in your house may have come to you simply because you have a spare room. But suppose this is the first time you're thinking about it or perhaps you haven't considered all of the possibilities. In addition to the traditional spare bedroom, there are a few other spaces that may work for you as a rental in your own house.

Master bedroom suite

If your house has a master bedroom suite with a private bathroom, this could make the ideal room rental. It may be dependent on your having another bedroom to use as an alternate master bedroom and your willingness to give up the master suite. The advantage of renting this room out is that it is self-contained with its own bathroom. It makes for a very attractive rental and avoids you and/or your family having to share a bathroom with the renter. In single-story houses where there is outside access from the master suite, say through a patio door, you could arrange for the tenant to have his or her private access, further reducing access to your house.

Finished basement

A finished basement with its own bathroom and private entrance is perhaps the ideal arrangement in a room rental situation. A basement rental with a private entrance minimizes renter access to the house and provides the greatest degree of privacy to you. Even if the basement has no direct outside entrance and your renter has to go through the house, a basement rental still provides a fair degree of privacy for renter and owner.

You have an obligation to only rent safe space to a tenant. Before you rent basement space, make sure it's in compliance with all applicable laws.

Lower level in a split-level or high ranch

This is similar to renting basement space except that it's unlikely to be completely closed off from the rest of the house or have its own entrance. One possibility here is to permit entry through the garage if, as in many high ranches, the garages are under the house next to the lower level.

The other major downside to renting the lower level in a split-level or high ranch is that this space is often part of very active living space for the family. This may prove an unacceptable inconvenience as a change in lifestyle. On the positive side, this space may be relatively private and large. It may even be divided into two or more rooms that, in effect, could be a small apartment.

Two bedrooms isolated from the rest of the house

Your house may have two unused bedrooms that are somewhat isolated from the rest of the other bedrooms. These could be rented out as a suite. Since the rooms have some privacy, the tenant could go between them without penetrating the rest of the house. Ideally, there would be a bathroom nearby. If you can spare the space, this arrangement could be very attractive to a renter who perhaps wanted a bedroom and living room.

Close off a main room

There are houses that have one or more of the principal living spaces such as the living room or dining room located as separate rooms with doors that effectively close the room off from the rest of the house. There is no question that access would have to be through the house unless there was a patio door or similar outside entrance directly into the room. In houses that have family rooms or great rooms, the living room and dining room are often seldom used. Even though this may not be the first place that comes to mind when you think of renting a room in your house, such arrangements can work very well.

Rent the house; live in the basement

Under specific circumstances renting out your house as detailed in the rest of this book while living in your basement may make more sense than you think. The key is the configuration of the basement and the number of people in your family. If you are one or two people and the basement has sufficient room for you, this may be the ideal temporary solution.

You can get much higher rent for the house than for a basement room. You can probably live with some physical situation that would make the rental difficult. You pay no rent. To keep things legal and safe, you'll still need to comply with all building and zoning codes as well as most likely share cooking facilities. But if you can work through those issues, living in your basement for a while may fit your needs.

Find a Renter

One of the best, if not the easiest ways, to find a renter is through friends and family. If that's not possible, keep in mind the kind of person who might find a single-room rental in your house attractive and focus your efforts to attract that person. If you live near a college or university, the campus is a natural place to advertise.

While you may be reluctant to rent your house to several college students, you should be less concerned about renting a room to one student. If the school is large enough to have professional and graduate schools, focus on those since you will be targeting a generally older student. Emphasize the quiet nature of the house and the room.

Find out if there is a writing program at the school. For the right price, you might attract a writer who needs a quiet space to write the great American novel.

When seeking a renter from a school, contact the school's housing office. They sometimes maintain referral lists of off-campus housing. Alternately, contact the student activities office and if necessary obtain permission to put your notice on the campus bulletin boards.

If you don't have a school nearby but there's a hospital in your town, try advertising there. You might contact the nursing supervisor or hospital director's office and ask advice as to how to get the word out that you have a room for rent.

Finally, an ad in the daily or weekly newspaper and the local free papers may get you results.

Decide the Terms of Your Rental

Following are a number of important decisions you'll need to make before advertising your room for rent:

- To have these terms and conditions in place
- To advertise the room rental accordingly
- To make the tenant clear on the conditions when they move in
- To enforce them thereafter

Do some research and think through your options in order to determine what to charge for rent. The expectations for the market and your own limits as to what you can live with will dictate the terms and conditions under which you will rent a room in your house.

To find out what the expectations of the market are, check out ads in the local newspapers. If you intend to go the college route as suggested previously, talk to the college housing office or someone in student activities and find out what the expectations are, including the rent, for a room rental. You'll want to ask about most of the issues discussed in the following sections.

As for your own likes and dislikes, you'll have to think through what are the "deal breakers" and on what things you can compromise. As you do your research and make your decisions, create a list that you can refer to when you write your advertisement. This list can also serve as the basis for your list of house rules that can be given to the new tenant.

Rent

The rent on a room is typically calculated and paid on a weekly basis. It is all-inclusive; that is, there are generally no other separate charges. The agreement can be as simple as a verbal agreement, supplemented by a list of rules, or a letter agreement. It should clearly state what the rental fee includes. Be clear when the rent is due and in what form—check, cash, money order. It is a good idea to obtain a week's rent in advance to compensate for the possibility of the tenant moving out without paying the last week's rent.

Number of People

Decide the maximum number of people you want to rent to. A single-room rental is usually limited to one person. If the tenant is someone you know or are related to and needs a few months' temporary quarters, you may allow a couple. If you decide you can rent a space larger than a single room, rental to two people may be more feasible. Since the space will not have a kitchen, a family rental may not be appropriate unless you are prepared to tolerate different eating habits.

Relationship

This question arises if the space you intend to rent out can accommodate two people. It is a fair housing question. You may have personal, religious, or moral objections to certain living arrangements between two people. The federal fair housing law is silent on this subject. State and local fair housing laws in some cases have addressed these issues. In most cases the owner-occupant who rents a room in his or her house is exempt from these laws.

Before you decide to rent to two people, determine if you have any problems with certain living arrangements. If so, check out your local fair housing laws to determine first, if that particular issue is a protected class, and second, if you are exempt as an owner-occupant-landlord.

Gender

The gender of the renter can be important to some people, depending on the amount of privacy the renter and the landlord will have from each other. A single owner of either sex may only want to rent a room to someone of the same gender. In this case, even though gender is a protected class in federal fair housing law, an exception is made for the owner-occupant-landlord. You should double-check your state and local laws if gender is going to be an issue for you.

Visitors

The possibilities with respect to visitors are:

- No visitors
- Visitors only in "public" space
- Same gender only
- Limited to one at a time
- Limited hours—days, evenings, overnight

In today's world, limiting visitors by gender is impractical. However, you may want to limit visitors to one at a time, before 11:00 P.M., and absolutely no overnight visitors to keep things under control. Your concerns are primarily noise and behaviors you don't wish to condone in your house.

Kitchen and Cooking Privileges

Many room rentals come with some sort of kitchen and cooking privileges. Permission is granted as part of the rental arrangement for the tenant to store food in the refrigerator and to use the kitchen appliances and utensils to prepare meals. Room renters often eat many of their meals outside the house.

The issue of kitchen privileges is a personal matter and should relate to your own lifestyle and privacy issues. Consideration should also be given to the market expectations for this type of room rental. Part of the consideration of the food issue is whether to permit eating in the room. Keep a watchful eye out for food and dirty dishes left in the room. Also make sure the trash container from the room is emptied frequently. Do not permit any cooking in the room. Hot plates, microwave ovens, and toasters all present fire hazards.

Meals

Depending on the situation, you may want to offer meals with the rental—most likely, limited to breakfast and dinner. Most room rentals do not come with meals; in your community this might be typical. If you offer meals, make clear when meals are served. You can ask the renter as a courtesy to advise you if she won't be taking a meal with you but don't expect too much in the way of advance notice.

Bathroom

If the room has its own bathroom, bathroom problems are minimized. Bathroom use issues will also be practically nonexistent if you have a sufficient number of bathrooms for the rest of the people in the house. But if you have one or two bathrooms for several family members plus the renter, you should address bathroom use.

The primary issue is scheduling. Renters certainly have a right to use the bathroom when necessary. At the same time, family schedules should not be overly disrupted by a renter's presence. It's a good idea to give renters a general idea of the family's schedule for extended bathroom use, for example, in the morning when most people are getting ready for school and work. You may want to prohibit renters from leaving anything in the bathroom and remind them of the expectation to leave the bathroom as they found it.

Laundry and Linens

Providing personal laundry service and/or permitting use of the washing machine and dryer is optional. Providing fresh bed linens and towels is generally included in the rent. Bed linen changes should be done at least weekly on a regular schedule. You may collect the used linens and make the bed yourself or simply provide the fresh linens to the renter and have him change them.

Daily bedmaking need not be included as part of the rent.

Fresh towels can be provided daily or every other day. Be aware of the practical issue of the renter having a wet towel that he cannot leave in the bathroom. You may want to provide a small towel rack in the room.

Cleaning

Cleaning should be included in the rental. Basic dusting, vacuuming, and mopping needs to be done on your regular cleaning schedule. It is inappropriate and probably foolish for you to expect any level of cleaning from the renter. You should advise the renter of when you will be cleaning the room and ask that the floors and surfaces be as neat as possible to facilitate cleaning.

Locks and Curfews

It will be difficult to rent a room with a curfew attached. You may like the feeling of having the house locked up and secure for the night after a certain time, but you are renting a room to an adult, not running a summer camp for children.

Give the renter a key to at least one door in the house. If you have an alarm system, discuss how that will work. For practical purposes, you may give the renter the key code and advise that after a certain hour, the alarm system will be on; they will need to use the code and reset the alarm if they come in after that time. For security purposes, change the key code at the end of the renter's term. You may also want to change the lock for which the renter has a key, even if the key has been returned.

Smoking

This is very much up to you. If you don't permit smoking, be sure the renter understands this and that the rule will also apply to all the renter's guests.

Drinking

Again this is very much up to you. The occasional solitary glass of wine or beer is probably of no harm, but drinking nonstop with the visitor who is there for a few hours can be problematic for everyone. My recommendation would be to initially ban alcohol and see what happens. If the renter seems to occasionally sneak in a beer or bottle of wine you can also choose to ignore it. The rule is in place should you need to enforce it if the issue becomes more serious.

Noise

Noise for your purposes would be any sound that can be heard outside of the rented room with the door closed. This could be TV, radio, music, musical instruments, or conversation. Set a time for no more noise, advise the renter when she moves in, and enforce the rule. You can also ask the renter to keep the noise to a minimum at other times of the day.

Put It Together

If you are not in a position to move or simply don't want to move yet, renting a room in your home may be a good compromise toward making a little money while waiting to sell your house. Renting a room in your house makes for very close living arrangements. Remember to always treat the landlord-renter relationship as a business even if you are only renting out a bedroom.

CHAPTER SEVENTEEN ACTION POINTS

- ☐ Check out the laws for renting a room in your house.

- ☐ Make some decisions about your privacy issues.

- ☐ Keep security in mind.

- ☐ Be creative about what space you can rent.

- ☐ Use networking and directed marketing to find a renter.

- ☐ Make all your decisions about the terms of your rental before you start advertising.

- ☐ Make sure the rules are clear to the renter and that you enforce them consistently.

CHAPTER EIGHTEEN

BECOME A REAL ESTATE INVESTOR

NOW THAT YOU'VE read through this book and perhaps are renting out your house, the idea of being a real estate investor may be appealing. You certainly know a lot more about the pros and cons of owning and managing an investment property, even if you had not expected to become a landlord. Following are some of the considerations in being a real estate investor.

First Decisions

There are two decisions you'll have to make at the starting point of becoming a real estate investor. The first concerns the kind of property to invest in, and the second concerns whether to be a landlord. Virtually any property that is rentable is a potential investment property. From single-family houses to shopping malls and from small office buildings to farmland—all of these can be purchased for the returns they will generate when rented for others to use.

The decision of what kind of property to invest in usually is limited by the money available for the investment and the expertise and comfort level of the investor, especially if the investor is thinking of self-managing the investment property.

Most people with no real estate investment background start with some type of residential property. The logic of this seems to be that people live in houses and apartments and in a sense know something already about managing them. The other concern is obtaining and dealing with tenants. And tenants are basically people like us.

Nonresidential space is usually more complex to manage and commercial tenants have very different needs from residential tenants. Without personal expertise, you are advised to use a management professional for nonresidential buildings of any size. An exception to this might be the small mixed-use building found in many urban and developed suburban areas, such as a building with one or two apartments over a commercial space. Generally these can be owner-managed with perhaps a small amount of advice or additional expertise needed to deal with the nonresidential tenant.

A decision to become a real estate investor is unavoidably linked to the management decisions. Small residential properties, the kind new investors often buy, generally do not generate enough income to permit the hiring of professional property managers. The decision to invest in this type of property is also usually a decision to be a landlord.

Form an Investment Group

As you prepare to become a real estate investor, you may want to consider whether to form an investment group. Advantages include having a larger amount of money to invest and shared responsibility. The disadvantages are less control and shared decision-making. Depending on who the other investors are, there could also be the risk of personal or family relationships getting in the way of the investment or vice versa.

When investing with other people, consider these key issues that should be resolved in the appropriate legal documents:

Ownership interest

Control/management

Tax benefits

Ability to sell the property

Distribution of assets upon dissolution

Liability

Profit sharing

There are many legal issues that will be part of whatever legal structure you create to own the property. The previous list will be a starting point when you speak with an attorney and your accountant about the various ways to legalize the relationship among members of an investment group.

There are a number of legal forms of association when two or more people want to do something together, such as own real estate. In addition to consulting professionals for general advice, ask about the following:

- Corporations—maintain control, limit liability, but may cause double taxation
- General partnership—shared control and liability
- Limited partnership—maintain control but limit tax advantages to the partners
- Limited Liability Corporation—may limit double taxation and may maintain control depending on how it's structured

The previous list is designed to stimulate conversation with the professionals you consult. Corporations are frequently used to limit individual personal liability in real estate ownership situations. Some owners will form a separate corporation for each building they own in order to protect the assets of one building from being used to pay off a lawsuit against another building.

Leverage

Leverage is one of the keys to making money on a real estate investment. It is the use of borrowed money to extend the impact of the cash you have available to invest. You probably borrowed money through a mortgage loan to buy your house. That's leverage. Chapter 19, "Real Estate Math," contains a few calculations that show the impact of leverage on a real estate investment.

Financing

Once you've determined how much money you have to invest, consult with the mortgage representatives of several different banks. They will help you determine the price of the investment property you can afford. This will be a rough estimate since a portion of the income from the investment will be counted in the calculation toward paying expenses. These estimates will be more accurate if you have already identified a possible property.

It is impossible to tell what any particular lender will be willing to lend on a specific property. In light of the recent mortgage crisis, lending institutions have made it more difficult to obtain mortgage loans. That is not to say that it has become impossible. An investor with a good credit score interested in purchasing a property that appears to be financially sound can still get a loan. The loan may not be the same as one obtained a few years ago but mortgage money is still available for investment properties.

Expect that the amount of down payment for an investment property will be higher than to buy a home to live in. Also, only a portion of the rents will be counted as income. The exact percentages in both cases will vary from bank to bank and will depend on the current credit market.

Select a Property

Most new real estate investors choose residential properties in which to invest. You've lived in a house and have a good idea of what it takes to manage one. Perhaps you've also been a tenant so you have a feel for what a tenant is looking for when renting an apartment or a house. Remember that the more units you have, the more easily you can financially weather a vacancy. On the other hand, too large a building will be difficult for you to manage yourself. If you want to go beyond owning one-family homes, anything between a two- and eight-unit apartment building is a good place to start.

Another option are small commercial buildings with rental apartments. Many older and smaller communities have buildings with storefront-type space on the first floor and one of more apartments on the second and third floors. Depending on the economic situation in the neighborhood, these can be good investments since you get a bit of both worlds—commercial and residential.

Finally, try to locate a property that is easily accessible for you. This is crucial when you are going to manage the property yourself. Even if you have a resident superintendent or janitor, it's important to keep a watchful eye on the building and the neighborhood.

Analyzing Income and Expenses

Earlier this book gave you a brief lesson in preparing a pro forma or projection of income and expenses. You can follow that outline and learn more from some basic books about real estate investing. Be realistic about the numbers when making projections. Real estate investments are too expensive and important to approach the decision emotionally.

When you analyze a property that you're thinking of buying, do the analysis a few times using different numbers. Project high rents and low expenses and then project low rents and high expenses. Don't forget a projection for vacancies. Ignore the tax benefits; then include the tax benefits. Analyze the property under various financial scenarios. If the property is a good investment with low rents, high expenses, and no tax benefits, it will be a great investment if you can keep expenses down and the rents go up.

Get the Information You Need to Analyze the Property

In an ideal world you'll be able to get two to three years' income and expense statements from the property owner. These are available since they had to be completed each year for tax purposes. If the owner is reluctant to give you anything but the past year, you have to wonder what he may be trying to hide—like large maintenance bills in previous years that he may have deferred last year in an attempt to make the financial statement of the property look better.

The other piece of helpful information will be more difficult to obtain: income and expense statements from other properties similar to the one you're considering. The place to go for these is to your real estate agent. Compare the property you're researching with other similar properties. For example, if most of the other properties use 2,000 gallons of oil per year for heat, investigate why the property you're considering uses 3,000 gallons per year and if that's something you can change if you buy the property.

Use the Professionals
As you consider making your first—and any—real estate investment, consult with the following:

- Real estate agent—especially one who specializes in small investment properties
- Attorney
- Accountant
- General property inspector
- Specialized inspectors, if appropriate (e.g., termite, radon, well and septic, engineer)

Money spent in making a wise choice and handling the transaction correctly will pay off in the long run.

Slow and Steady Wins the Race
The wisest investors I know try to make some money each year from their real estate investments. They take advantage of tax benefits but don't count on them. They hope for an appreciation in the price of the property when they sell it, but they don't plan on it. Some investors even take the position that as long as all the

expenses for the property can be paid out of the property's income, they will be able to sell the property free and clear of all mortgage debt if they hold it long enough.

The purchase of any investment property to some degree is speculation on the future. We hope rents will go up faster than expenses; we hope for full occupancy rates; we hope for rising property values. These speculations on the future are inevitable.

The riskiest form of speculation for real estate investment in my opinion is what might be called the fast turnaround. You buy a property in a fast-rising market in hopes that the immediate past appreciation in property values will continue. You plan to sell the property in a few years and make a substantial profit. In some cases the rents can barely pay the bills. Or you might own a property with a negative cash flow and have to put money into the property each month to pay the expenses. Your hope is that you'll be able to sell it at a price that will cover this monthly contribution plus yield a substantial profit. When this strategy works, it's great. The problem with this approach is that it banks on a future that is usually too distant to discern with any degree of certainty.

Instead, try to:

- Buy good properties after careful analysis.
- Buy properties that yield a reasonable annual return on your investment.
- Hold the properties for as long as it is feasible when values are steady or rising in the neighborhood.
- Sell or refinance properties as appropriate to expand your holdings.
- Think long term in terms of estate building for your own future and that of your family.

Use What You've Learned

Becoming a landlord may have been a surprise. If you're reading this chapter and giving it serious consideration, then it appears that becoming a landlord was a pleasant surprise.

Real estate is still considered a good way to build long-term wealth. It is a way to achieve financial independence from a salaried job. It's a way to provide income for retirement, children's educations, and any other financial obligation that usually requires long-term financial planning.

CHAPTER EIGHTEEN ACTION POINTS

☐ Decide if you are cut out to be a real estate investor.

☐ Determine how much money you have to invest.

☐ Think about forming an investment group.

☐ Look at and analyze a number of properties.

☐ Inform yourself through research and the use of professionals such as real estate brokers.

CHAPTER NINETEEN

REAL ESTATE MATH

THIS CHAPTER PROVIDES you with some examples of the calculations mentioned throughout this book. Some of these will help you decide whether or not to rent your house, set a rental rate, and do a pro forma, and a few formulas should help you manage your rental.

Making the Decision to Rent Your House—Negative Cash Flow Rental

It's not practical to cover all of the mathematical variables that might go into a decision to rent versus sell your house. One issue you should consider if you can't rent the house for enough to cover your house costs is renting versus selling. Here is an example:

Current sale price of house	$300,000
Desired sale price of house	$400,000
Estimated inflation/appreciation rate	5% per year
Monthly house expenses (mortgage, taxes, insurance—tenant pays all others)	$2,200
Expected monthly rent	$1,700

The steps are outlined on the following page.

Future sale price of house – Current sale price of house =
Expected Difference

$400,000 – $300,000 = $100,000

Expected difference / Future sale price =
Approximate difference as a percentage

$100,000/$400,000 = 25 percent

Percentage difference / (Appreciation/Inflation) rate =
Number of years house is to be rented

25 percent / 5 percent = 5 years

Years to be rented x 12 months = Months to be rented

5 x 12 = 60

Due to the compounding of inflation / appreciation rates and trying to keep this simple, the number of years/months is a close approximation. In fact, at a 5 percent per year inflation/appreciation rate, it will take more than five but less than six years to reach $400,000.

House expenses – Rent = Negative cash flow

$2,200 – $1,700 = $500

Negative cash flow x Number of months house is rented =
Out of pocket

$500 x 60 = $30,000

Expected difference in house price – Out of pocket =
What you make by waiting to sell

$100,000 – 30,000 = $70,000

This is still a tidy profit from waiting but perhaps not as much as you expected. Obviously, the result depends on many assumptions and the specific numbers you have to work with. If you can rent the property for more than your expenses, you can skip this altogether.

But if you're in a negative cash flow situation, try this one with your numbers. You should also note that the prediction for rising house prices (inflation/appreciation) will be particular to your area.

Making the Decision to Rent Your House— Your Living Expenses

To analyze the situation where you become a renter while your house is being rented and waiting to be sold, use this formula:

Number of months you rent × Cost of rent

If you have to rent a house or apartment at say $1,000 per month for the sixty months calculated in the previous example that it will take to sell your house, your total rental cost will be:

60 × $1,000 = $60,000

If you combine this with the Out of Pocket total from the previous example of $30,000, you arrive at a total of $90,000. At this point you've reduced your profit from waiting to sell to $10,000.

These two examples paint a bleak financial picture of renting your house because you assume substantial losses and costs. But now that you've got a feel for the formulas, suppose the situation were reversed. You are able to rent your house at a monthly profit of $300 (that is $300 positive cash flow above your expenses) and you can live with family either for free or for say $200 per month. Using the other assumptions, you will make the additional $100,000 on the sale of the house plus $6,000 for the sixty months the house was rented and essentially live rent-free.

Commissions

Basic real estate commissions are calculated as a percentage.

Sale price x Commission rate = Commission owed
$300,000 x 5 percent = $15,000

Monthly rent x Commission rate = Commission owed
$1,600 x 25 percent = $400

Note that commission rates are for illustrative purposes only and are always subject to negotiation. Real estate agents sometimes charge one or more months' rent as a commission. Depending on your market area and the agreement made, the tenant might be responsible for the commission on a rental.

Pro Forma

Here is a simple pro forma using annual figures:

Potential Gross Income	$12,000
Vacancy and Collection Loss*	$1,000
Effective Gross Income	$11,000

Fixed Expenses	
Taxes	$3,000
Insurance	$400
Variable Expenses**	$1,200
Reserves	$500
Total Expenses	$5,100

Net Operating Income	$5,900
Mortgage Payment***	$5,900
Cash Flow	$0

*One month's rent.
** Do not include expenses paid by tenant.
***Principle and interest.

Analyzing Comparable Properties

You learned in Chapter 8 to do a general analysis of comparables that may be different from your property. With comparables that are similar, you should find the mean or average and the median. Say you've located five rental houses that are very similar to yours and the monthly rents are as follows:

$1,500 $1,600 $1,300 $1,400 $1,500

You get the average by adding up all the numbers and dividing by the number of numbers.

1,500 + 1,600 + 1,300 + 1,400 + 1,500 = 7,300
7,300 / 5 = 1,460

The median is $1,500, which is the middle number if you arrange the numbers in ascending order:

$1,300 $1,400 $1,500 $1,500 $1,600

If there were six numbers, you would take an average of the middle two numbers.

When numbers are grouped closely together as these were, the average or mean is probably just as good as the median. But if one of these rents was very high or very low, it would skew the average, so the median would be a better indicator of what the group of numbers is telling you.

Given the two numbers just calculated, you should probably look a little further into the comparables to see if you could justify a $1,500 per month rental or if your house is closer in comparability to a $1,400 rental.

Leverage

As a homeowner already you probably understand leverage but since it was mentioned in the chapter on becoming an investor, a quick review is warranted. The concept used in leverage is called the Loan to Value ratio or LTV, which is the amount a lender will loan you as a percentage of the value (not the price) of the property. It is the reverse of the required down payment. If the bank requires a 20 percent down payment to buy a property, they are offering you a loan with an LTV of 80 percent.

Value x LTV = Loan amount

Say you are looking at a property whose value (generally estimated in an appraisal) is $500,000 and the bank is offering a loan with an LTV of 80 percent.

$500,000 × 80 percent = $400,000 Mortgage loan amount

$500,000 − $400,000 = $100,000 Down payment

There are two other calculations about the effects of leverage on an investment that have to do with profit and return. Suppose after a few years you are able to sell your investment property for $550,000. That's a profit of $50,000.

$550,000 − $500,000 = $50,000

That appears to be a profit of 10 percent:

$50,000 / $500,000 = 10 percent

But, in fact, this is the correct calculation:

$50,000 / $100,000 = 50 percent

The key here is that you actually only invested $100,000 of your money not the entire $500,000. So you made the $50,000 profit on $100,000 of your money.

The same type of calculation works for annual cash flow. Say on this investment you have a cash flow of $10,000 per year. You're making that on the $100,000 investment and not on the entire $500,000 cost of the property. You are making 10 percent.

$10,000 / $100,000 = 10 percent

Any profits are subject to taxes, but these calculations give you an idea of the benefits of leverage when investing in real estate.

Late Fee for Late Rental Payment

If you are going to charge a late fee for late rental payments, check with local laws for maximum amounts that can be charged. Rather than a percentage, use a rounded number. For example, let's say the rent is $1,100 per month and the local law says you can charge a late fee of up to 4 percent of the rent.

$1,100 × 4 percent = $44

I would round this down to $40 at the maximum and state it as such in the lease rather than stating a percentage.

Lease with an Option to Buy—Credit for Rent

Following is an example of this. Assumptions:

Sale price of the property agreed to in option	$400,000
Monthly rent	$1,200
Credit to be given toward purchase price	$500 per month
Length of time the house is rented	28 months

28 × $500 = $14,000

$400,000 − $14,000 = $386,000 (Amount owed by tenant to purchase the property.)

In effect, the tenant has already paid you $14,000 toward the purchase price.

Market Conditions

Analyzing and predicting market conditions is difficult and imprecise. It may be helpful, however, to try to understand what's going on in your market. Look at current inventory and compare it to how many houses sell over a given period of time.

Here's a simple formula:

Number of houses on the market / Current market absorption rate
= Amount of inventory

Assumptions:

Number of houses currently on the market	800
Number of houses currently being sold monthly	20

800 / 20 = 40 months of inventory
(assumes no new houses come on the market in that time)

Now do the same comparison with numbers from two or three years ago. You'll probably find many more houses on the market and a lower absorption rate. This does not mean that it will take you forty months to sell your house, but it may take longer than it would have a few years ago.

The other issue currently affecting market conditions is the large number of foreclosures in various markets. These are generally viewed as a separate segment of the market due to their relatively low prices. It is likely that the foreclosures in your area will have to sell before your house will command a reasonable price. Real estate prices are comparable in any given market. If someone can purchase a house just like yours at a "foreclosure price," they will want your house at that price. Determining how many foreclosures are on the market in your area will also help you judge when the market might improve.

The numbers for these calculations are most likely available from your local real estate board or chamber of commerce. In fact, they may have already done the calculations.

REFERENCES

General books on being a landlord; some containing lease and other forms:

Butler, Mike. *Landlording on Autopilot*. Hoboken, NJ: John Wiley and Sons, 2006.

Garrison, Marc Stephan, and Tripp-Garrison, Paula. *Unlimited Real Estate Profit*. Avon, MA: Adams Media, 2004.

Griswold, Robert. *Property Management for Dummies*. Hoboken, NJ: Wiley Publishing, Inc., 2001.

Roberson, Cliff. *The Landlord's Book of Forms and Agreements*. New York: McGraw-Hill, 2006.

Robinson, Leigh. *Landlording*. 10th ed. El Cerrito, CA: ExPress, 2006.

Roth, Ken. *The Successful Landlord*. New York: American Management Association (AMACOM), 2004.

Tremore, Judy. *The Everything® Landlording Book*. Avon, MA: Adams Media, 2005.

Weiss, Mark B, and Baldwin, Dan. *Landlording & Property Management*. Avon, MA: Adams Media, 2003.

Websites for lease forms

Note: Be sure to use a state-specific form or modify a standard form to meet your state's requirements.

www.LawDepot.com
www.publiclegalforms.com
www.AgreementsEtc.com
www.FindLegalForms.com
www.FindThatQualityTenant.com
www.RealDealDocs.com
www.USLegalForms.com
www.rentalcashflow.com
www.lectlaw.com

Websites for houses/apartments for rent to advertise your property and/or do comparative rent analysis

www.Rent.com
www.Pronto.com
www.MyNewPlace.com
www.rentals.com
www.housesforrent.ws
www.Rentspeeed.com
www.rentalads.com
www.RentalHouses.com

Credit reporting agencies

www.equifax.com
www.experian.com
www.transunion.com

Criminal background research

www.GovernmentRegistry.org
www.CourtRecords.org
www.Reverserecords.org

Federal fair housing laws
www.hud.gov

Federal tax laws
www.irs.gov

Property management
www.irem.com

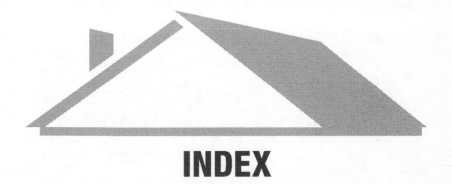

INDEX

ABOUT THE AUTHOR

JOHN A. YOEGEL, PHD, has been an instructor on a variety of real estate topics for more than twenty years. In addition to his doctorate and a professional master's degree in urban planning he holds the Distinguished Real Estate Instructor designation from the Real Estate Educators Association. This designation is held by fewer than 125 real estate instructors throughout the nation. He is a licensed real estate broker in New York State and is the former Director of Real Estate for Westchester County, New York. This is his fifth real estate book. John lives with his wife Marina in New Fairfield, Connecticut, where in their spare time they make award winning wines.

John would be happy to hear from his readers and their experiences as a result of the advice in this book. He can be reached through the publisher.

MOMENTS MATTER

How One Defining Moment Can Create a Lifetime of Purpose

DAVE SANDERSON
Miracle on the Hudson Passenger
WITH CINDY WRIGHTSON

First Edition: 1.2 April 2016
ISBN-13: 978-0692618530
Printed in the United States of America
Jacket design by Ilian
Front and back jacket photograph by Janis Krums
Photographs of Dave Sanderson by Allie Miller
Published by: AbundantPress.com

Abundant Press
Publish · Promote · Profit · Position · Platform
AbundantPress.com